CELIBACY —
GIFT OR LAW?

A Critical Investigation

HEINZ-J. VOGELS

With a Foreword by
ADRIAN HASTINGS

Sheed & Ward

This translation first published in Great Britain in 1992 by Burns & Oates, Wellwood, North Farm Rd., Tunbridge Wells, Kent TN2 3DR.

Published originally in Germany by Kösel Verlag, Munich, under the title *Pflichtzölibat* in 1978, revised edition 1992 by Köllen Verlag, Bonn. This translation of the original edition was made by G.A. Kon, revised and augmented by the author in collaboration with Guy Moore and Paul Burns.

Original edition© Kösel Verlag 1978, Köllen Verlag 1992

This edition© 1993 by Sheed & Ward

Sheed & Ward™ is a service of The National Catholic Reporter Publishing Company.

Library of Congress Cataloguing in Publication Data

Vogels, Heinz-Jürgen.
    [Pflichtzölibat. English]
    Celibacy : gift or law? / Heinz-J. Vogels ; with a foreword by Adrian Hastings.
       p.   cm.
    Translation of: Der Pflichtzölibat.
    Includes bibliographical references.
    ISBN 1-55612-653-0 (alk. paper)
    1. Celibacy--Catholic Church--Controversial literature. 2. Celibacy (Canon law) 3. Catholic Church--Doctrines. 4. Catholic Church--Clergy--Sexual behavior. I. Title.
BV4390.V5813   1993
253'.2--dc20

                                                   93-19235
                                                   CIP

Published by: Sheed & Ward
                115 E. Armour Blvd.
                P.O. Box 419492
                Kansas City, MO 64141

To order, call: (800) 333-7373

Cover design by Tim Botts

Contents

Foreword

The Catholic Church is at present tearing itself to pieces over the issue of the law of clerical celibacy. It might seem to some only a marginal or administrative problem but it in fact goes to the heart of the matter on every side of modern church life. It is, of course, first of all an issue of sexuality, originally deriving from a belief that all sex produces moral impurity. But it has gone on to become an issue about power, about pastoral care, and about sheer honesty: power, because the desire of Catholics in many parts of the world is now overwhelmingly to be allowed to have married priests as well as celibate ones but Roman authority refuses to listen; pastoral care, because tens of thousands of able priests have left the ministry on account of the law and a real eucharistic famine is spreading from Africa, Latin America and the Philippines even to Europe and the United States; sheer honesty because it has become overwhelmingly clear that the law is not kept well in many parts of the world and that in consequence a great deal of duplicity and imposed silence has been required. Today the pretence has broken down to be replaced increasingly by a destructive incredulity.

The publication in English of Heinz-J. Vogels' scholarly study of the subject is immensely to be welcomed. It is timely. It is learned. It is also extremely respectful of Catholic tradition. Vogels is in no way a theological radical. It is from the viewpoint not of a scoffing secular world but of a deeply committed, quite conservative Catholicism that he demonstrates how mistaken the present law certainly is. It does not reflect the gospel or the early church but a medieval aberration which is now strangling the life of a church which can no longer benefit from pretending to remain part of the middle ages. He goes out of his way to stress the evangelical value of celibacy but as charism not as law – indeed the obligation of law actually destroys the effective value of the charism. Finally, he argues, rightly I believe, that as a law it is simply invalid. It fails to fulfil the conditions of a just law and priests can not be bound by it.

It is greatly to be hoped that the reading of this book will help to bring about, and rapidly, a major change, for without a new pattern of priestly ministry uniting the married with the celibate, the future for the church can only be an immensely depressing one.

ADRIAN HASTINGS

Introduction

Compulsory celibacy has come under tremendous pressure. As a consequence the question of celibacy itself has also often been raised. It is not the purpose of this book to cast doubt on the value of celibacy. Rather, I should emphasize at the outset that celibacy for the sake of heaven is a high value which has proved to contribute to the expansion of the Kingdom, and which must be upheld and retained in the Church. Nothing should or will be said against those religious who, for reasons of calling and inclination, choose a celibate life, nor against priests who voluntarily live their lives in an unmarried, celibate state. They have been endowed with a special gift from God: the capacity for celibacy. Indeed, they have received two callings, one to the priesthood and one to celibacy.

There is, however, another group that combines the calling to the priesthood and the calling to marriage. About 20 percent of serving Catholic priests are married. These are the priests of the Eastern Catholic Churches in, for example, Hungary, Czechoslovakia, the Ukraine, Lebanon. . . . They fall under the jurisdiction of the pope, just as much as the priests of the Western Church, and may be married with his blessing.

The eventful past few years have seen the door to the East reopened, not only in political terms, but also in church terms. During a meeting with the Orthodox Patriarch of Constantinople, Pope John Paul II employed a wonderful image which has been much quoted since: the Church must breathe again with both its lungs, the Eastern and the Western, in order to rediscover its fullness.[1]

It is to just this end that these reflections hope to stimulate readers: to rediscover the comprehensive fullness, the "Catholic" body. Christ gave his Church the wealth of two charisms which can be connected to the vocation of parish priesthood: celibacy and marriage. Paul embodied the first state, Peter the second. Both were excellent apostles of the Lord and both endowed the Roman Church with their apostolic authority. And both should also be embodied in the legislation and life of the Roman Church. For the Western Church too can draw strength from the full richness of Jesus Christ. Indeed it must if it hopes to overcome the chronic shortage of priests for pastoral work and the incapacity of so many priests to live in celibacy.

The argumentation of this book aims to assist in reconsidering the concept of compulsory celibacy and replacing it with voluntary celibacy and the choice for priests to marry. The fullness that Christ wishes for his Church envisages the capacity for union of the three callings: the calling to the priesthood as a vocation on the one hand can be combined with the social callings of either celibacy or marriage on the other. It should also be possible for these two social callings to co-exist side by side, as is indeed the practice in the Eastern Church.

Those who wish to see celibacy maintained as a high value for priests are quite right in the esteem in which they hold this calling. But – and this is where we touch on the real problem involved in compulsory celibacy –

---

1. See *Osservatore Romano*, 23 June 1985, p.5.

the ability to live as a celibate is, as Jesus says, "not given to all", and celibacy is, therefore, not good for all.

Let us look at the subject matter of each chapter:

1. Because those "to whom it has been given" find it easy to remain unmarried, it is psychologically almost impossible for them to imagine the position of those who have not received the charism but who, nevertheless, face the demand of the law that they refrain from marriage. Throughout the centuries, the main difficulty with celibacy has been contained in this dilemma. Mutual understanding has been lacking because charismatics have been addressing non-charismatics. Now, since the work of Sigmund Freud and others, the human sciences have revealed what life is like for those who are not specifically called to celibacy but who, nevertheless, endeavour to maintain it. Such suppression of what has to be allowed to develop for the sake of maturity and ability to love, namely, their God-given disposition to be completed by a partner, often results in neurosis. And worse still, such suppression may even lead to aberrations such as paedophilia, adultery or promiscuity.

The fact that many priests have become neurotics or fallen short in their duties, despite prayer, sacraments and asceticism, is shown by the experience of many doctors and psychologists, as well as by the papal authorities' practice of dispensation applied since the Second Vatican Council.[2]

---

2. For the USA especially see the findings of Richard Sipe, *A Secret World: Sexuality and the Search for Celibacy* (New York, 1990). This study of twenty-five years shows that only 10 percent of the clergy have no problems with celibacy; every second American priest suffers from psychological immaturity or sexual difficulties. For facts worldwide, see David Rice, *Shattered Vows: The Exodus of Catholic*

The basic psychoanalytical tenet that neuroses are laid down in the mental traumas of earliest childhood does not contradict this. For many such obstacles are spontaneously disposed of as the child becomes an adult, at the latest in marriage if that person is called to it. It is true that neurotics are found among married people as well, but it is obvious that the continual compulsion to repress, dominating the mind and body of those obliged to remain celibate, is far more apt to develop an early childhood trauma into a neurosis.

The fact that many good and pious priests have become neurotics shows that prayer – proposed by the Council of Trent and the Second Vatican Council[3] as a solution in the dilemma of law and charism – is not practicable for everyone. The conciliar statement says: "Priests should ... (pray) for the gift of fidelity (in

Clergy (London, 1990). More than 80,000 priests have left the active ministry during the last twenty-five years.

According to the Congregation for the Doctrine of the Faith's _Procedural Regulations on Dispensation_ of 13 Jan. 1971: AAS 63 (1971), 303–8, here 304, renewed in 1980 and in force to the present, the investigation to be set in motion by the local bishop, concerning the priest seeking dispensation, is "to cover above all the grounds and circumstances of the difficulties with which the supplicant is surrounded: before ordination, problems such as illnesses, physical or mental immaturity; after ordination: errors concerned with celibacy and priesthood, loose morals and so on." The Congregation certainly did not intend to accept that the celibacy law can be the cause of immaturity and illnesses. Yet at least it indicated the the illnesses which are grounds for a dispensation. Cf. S. Leist, _Zum Thema Zölibat. Bekenntnisse von Betroffenen_ (Munich, 1979); U. Goldmann-Posch, _Unheilige Ehen_ (Munich, 1985).

3. _Concilium Tridentinum_, sessio 24, can. 9, in Denzinger-Schönmetzer, eds., _Enchiridion Symbolorum, Definitionum et Declarationum de rebus Fidei et Morum_ (DS) (Barcelona-Freiburg, etc., 34th ed., 1967) = DS 1809. Second Vatican Council, Decree on the Ministry and Life of Priests, _Presbyterorum Ordinis_ (PO), in W. Abbott, ed., _The Documents of Vatican II_ (Washington, DC and London, 1966), p. 567.

continence). It is never denied to those who ask". In practice this does not hold true. For it cannot be supposed that neurotic priests, or other priests for that matter, have not sought to keep to the law and have not prayed. On the contrary, they have become neurotics just because of their strong wish to take on the legal obligation. On the moral plane only liberals have no complexes – or those who have the spiritual gift, and they for other, positive reasons.

Priests can therefore be divided into two categories: On one hand the charismatic celibate empowered by God remains healthy in his celibacy simply because he has "the gift from God", which gives him the ability to achieve something unusual. On the other hand, those not blessed with this spiritual gift realize that even through constant prayer they will not receive the grace of the "ability not to marry" (Matt. 19:12), but will possibly become ill, because such a central function of life as is desire for intimate partnership and power to hand on life cannot be suppressed with impunity: *"Nátur(am) éxpellás furcá, tamen úsque recúrret"* (Horace, Ep.I.10,24). The only consequence they can draw from this experience is to conclude that they, in turn, have received the charism of marriage (1 Cor. 7:7).

The priests who break out of the straightjacket of the law (whether in secret like Bishop Bossuet, the famous preacher,[4] or openly as, since 1964, "secularized" priests have increasingly done, mainly on account of the celibate state), escape this consequence of falling ill. Those who, by grace, have stayed healthy in the celibate state can, however, only with difficulty put themselves in the place

---

4. LThK, 2. ed. II,624; G. Denzler, *Das Papsttum und der Amtzölibat*, vol. II (Päpste und Päpsttum 5,2, Stuttgart, 1976) p.265.

of those who have become ill through celibacy, and this forms the basis of mutual lack of understanding.

This practical experience is confirmed, on the one hand, by the violations of the law throughout the centuries (priests without the "gift" cannot keep to the law), and, on the other, by the harsh criticism of these "sinners" who, basically, only wanted to be healthy,[5] uttered out of incomprehension by office-holders endowed with the spiritual gift of celibacy. These practical experiences, then, throw up the theoretical problem of whether the statements of the Council of Trent and of Vatican II concerning the attainability of the charism by prayer, are valid. The fact that Trent placed this concept outside the actual anathema of canon 9 of the 24th session – namely in the appended explanation so that anyone who casts doubt on this phrase is not affected by the ban of the preceding condemnation[6] – may stand here as a preliminary argument in favour of such a doubt being possible and permissible.

So the first purpose of this study is to subject the thesis which Vatican II took over from Trent (which, as stated, can be challenged with impunity) – that the spiritual gift of celibacy can be obtained by prayer – to a critical examination from the point of view of the New Testament (chapter 1).

2. It must be stressed that all the laws on celibacy which the Latin Church has brought into force have, of course, been enacted in good faith as to their being founded on the Old and New Testaments. This fact, however, does

---

5. Denzler, I and II, *passim*.
6. This is the case with only three of the otherwise very numerous Tridentine canons: DS 1512–4. In DS 1661 a new statute is added on after the anathema, but no new reason.

not rule out the possibility of error in these laws on discipline, which would then be open to challenge. There is no lack of reverence in this statement, for only in its "teaching on faith and morals" is the Church, as a whole and especially as the successor of St Peter "in the case of *ex-cathedra* decisions, infallible".[7] In disciplinary questions it is just as fallible as any other human law-giver.

So the Church's infallibility is not called into question by saying that, on the evidence of the documents available and by general agreement in the publications cited, the laws governing the state of celibacy grew out of an understanding of sexuality on the part of the Church's law-givers that had not yet been penetrated by the leaven of faith.

This inadequate understanding still affects our times, as the documentation provided by Denzler[8] impressively proves: as recently as 2 February 1975, Pope Paul VI referred to the fact that unmarried priests and members of religious orders conserve "purity of the body", thereby indirectly stigmatizing the marital act as impure. This reflects the times of Popes Damasus I and Siricius, as shown in a letter from the latter to Himerius of Tarragona[9] dating from the year 385. The opposition of the highest office-holders in the Latin Church to a connection between the sacraments of ordination and marriage, is due, even nowadays, to a concept of marriage which has not yet fully integrated the biblical statements of Ephesians 5 and Hebrews 13 that marriage is holy and a sacrament.

---

7. DS 3073f; Vatican II, *Lumen gentium* 25d, in Abbott, p.49.
8. Denzler II,366. Quotation from *Osservatore Romano* (German edition), 14 Feb. 1975.
9. DS 185, more ample quotation in the old Denzinger 89. Denzler I, pp.12–19.

Yet as Paul says, only "whatever does not proceed from faith is sin" (Rom. 14:23); therefore no guilty intention attaches to the Church authorities of earlier centuries, even if their negligence in overlooking these biblical texts on the holiness of marriage, which should have prevented them from calling it impure, is hard to understand.

However, this judgment that Church authorities are not guilty may now change if the hierarchy and all the faithful become aware of the untenable motives which brought about the introduction of restraint within marriage in the fourth century (and restraint from marriage in the twelfth): the idea of cultic impurity found in the Old Testament, in those times misunderstood as a moral wickedness, and the more or less conscious motive of Hellenistic-Gentile hostility to the body.

If these motives are at work still and are not replaced by new ones, then the question arises whether the law is valid at all. For, nowadays at least, the theoretical legal standard applies to each and every law: "To enable it to be binding, the law must be morally good, or if it is neutral, take its moral goodness from its purpose or the immediate circumstances."[10] Motives of hostility to the body and to marriage, which must be seen as the reason for the law on celibacy as it existed up to 1918 (according to the evidence of the texts to be presented below), cannot be taken as providing a morally good purpose or circumstance, but only as the expression of something wrongly understood in its time. If no other convincing

---

10. K. Mörsdorf, *Lehrbuch des Kirchenrechts*, vol. I (Paderborn, 11th ed. 1964) p.84. Cf. B. Häring, *Das Gesetz Christi I* (Freiburg, 6th ed. 1961) pp.310, 313ff. Eng. trans. *The Law of Christ* (Westminster, Md, 1961).

justification and purpose have been given by the ecclesiastical authorities for the continuation of the law, then we really need to question whether the law ever achieved validity and whether it still remains binding.

This then is the the second major issue with which this study must be concerned: Are the grounds which Vatican II (PO 16) puts forward for the retention of the law in place of the original reasonable, morally good and just – all of which, according to Moersdorf (*loc. cit.*), are preconditions for a law to have binding force? It is a major requirement of a just law that it may not go against revelation and the *ius divinum*. How far, for instance, does the Council take account of the fact that a spiritual gift is necessary for a life of celibacy, a gift which is "given" only to a few, "not" to "all" (Matt. 19:11f)? Is it possible to support a law which is binding upon all? The Council itself says that celibacy "is not indeed demanded by the very nature of priesthood' (PO 16a). How then may it oblige all priests? The Council emphasizes the suitability of the celibate state for priests as the new reason for the law; but by imposing a general law on all priests it makes *de facto* and *de jure* necessity out of suitability and enforces obedience to the law by means of the heaviest sanctions. What about those priests who have not received the "gift", needed for celibacy, from God?

In reality, the situation of the Council was this: the old law, having had its origin in an earlier motivation, continues in existence; its former reasons are acknowledged as untenable; the new explanation by "befitting" (PO 16e) represents an attempt at justification through less debatable arguments; these, however, do not fit the law as it stands – gift and "befitting" might justify only a counsel to remain unmarried, never a general law.

As to the gift, the Council and, later, some of the bishops attempt to interpret the law as a principle of selection, as if Church leaders could use this law to accept as candidates for the priesthood only those who, after searching self-examination, can hope that they have the spiritual gift to remain unmarried.[11] However, such a law would have to be classified as one of what Canon Law calls "irregularities" or conditions of suitability for the office of priest. It is true that the simple, dispensable obstacle of being married is to be found there (can. 1042,1 CIC), but this is not a principle of selection. Rather, the relevant celibacy law is found, to the present day, among the "obligations" laid upon the clergy (Title III chapter III of Book II CIC, *De clericorum obligationibus*). Looking at this title one is forced to say that, according to the existing right (*de lege lata*) the law is not a principle of selection placed prior to admission to the priesthood but an obligation laid on the members of the profession, still inspired by the assumed incompatibility of marriage and priesthood. It is formally equated there with the other obligations of the calling, as for instance to say the breviary, to wear a particular dress, and not to undertake any business.[12] The simple mention of celibacy being a "gift" from God in the new Code of 1983 (can 277 §1)

11. Cf. *Zehn Thesen des Erzbischofs von Köln, Kardinal Josef Höffner, "Um des Himmelreiches willen, über den Zölibat der Priester"* (Themen und Thesen 1, Cologne, 6th ed. 1975, and following eds. to 1986), thesis VI, p.15. Pope John Paul II, Letter of Holy Thursday 1979 to Priests: AAS 72 (1980) p.1132 no.9.

12. Also according to the new rite of ordination, *Pontificale Romanum* (Rome, 1972) pp.29ff, celibacy is still an obligation which must be "adhered to". Candidates for priesthood are asked:*"Vultis caelibatum custodire?"* Pope Paul VI's introductory *Motu Proprio* of 18 Aug. 1972 speaks of an *"obligatio"* (!), not of charism.

does not solve the problem of how a gift can be imposed as an obligation.

3. The term "obligation" leads us to another factor in the complex problem of celibacy as a law: Can a human law-giver demand abstention from a natural right – which the Apostle Paul claims also to apply to the apostles and their helpers – namely, abstention from the right to marry? It becomes clear from this discrepancy alone that the law grew from other roots than the notion of "charism", the gift from God, or from spontaneously renouncing a natural right. Neither "befitting" nor "obligations of the profession" can justify totally depriving persons of their natural rights. Chapter 3 deals therefore with the natural right to be accompanied by a wife and the Apostle Paul's attitude to it (1 Cor. 9:5).

4. The further question then follows: Can the celibacy law then bind the conscience when its original basis and moral aim, the "purity of priests", has been recognized as mistaken and has seemingly not been replaced by any new basis on which to justify so far-reaching an obligation? Must it not be repealed? To quote Moersdorf again: "When the overt objective which the law-giver associated with his decree has disappeared, then it is true that the law does not yet formally cease to exist, but it has no further compelling force."[13] This is the old tag: *Cessante causa cessat lex.* If the objective of keeping priests from "impure" activity within marriage has disappeared – and in fact nobody dares to repeat the original motivation of the law – then we have to ask whether the law has any compelling force at present. Furthermore,

---

13. Mörsdorf I, p.119.

since it did not take account of the free will or the natural
and apostolic right of those affected, could it take away
a God-given right to be accompanied by a wife (1 Cor.
9,5)? The answer must be negative, because 'divine right'
is the highest category in canon law, to be respected by
any law-giver.

5. Finally, there remains the question whether the
Church, in future, could expressly set up the charism as
a principle of selection (*de lege ferenda*). Chapter 5 deals
with this crucial question: it would mean that Church
leaders could refuse vocations to the priesthood coming
from God. It is not very likely that it could be justified in
doing so.

6. Having dealt with this, what arguments speak
positively in favour of bringing together the sacraments
of ordination and marriage? This is the subject of
Chapter 6.

7. Pastoral considerations form the conclusion, in Chapter 7.

*   *   *

So exegetical, historical, canonical and dogmatic con-
diderations are all involved in solving the problem of
celibacy, and they demonstrate the law's interrelation
with almost all branches of theology. This shows why it
is so hard to untangle these problems.

Once again let me emphasize in concluding this
Introduction: my investigations are concerned only with
the problems of celibacy as a law. I have no objection to
celibacy as a gift from God; on the contrary: without
charismatics of celibacy like Mother Teresa and Brother

Roger Schutz, Bishop Helder Camara and many others, both Church and world would be much poorer, less Christian. Celibacy as unmarried life-style grows out of quite other motives than the law's obligation on the individual priest: for instance, from the divine gift felt present in one's soul, from the wish to be free for the service of God's Kingdom (Matt. 19:12; 1 Cor. 7:25–35), as testimony for the world to come (Heb. 9:11; Luke 20:35). The texts of the law as formulated, which became valid for the whole Latin Church, do not, however, manifest such motives. In them the prohibitive character of celibacy, based on the "purity" demanded of priests, is clearly dominant.

In the Old Covenant celibacy was a cultic necessity for priests during the days of their ministry within the temple. However, this cultic "impurity" arising from sexual acts wore off by itself through the passage of time, "in the evening" (Lev. 15:16). Early Christian tradition, however read from this a moral impurity in the coital act, which in turn appeared to require total abstinence from marriage and procreation, since Christian priests had to approach the altar every day.[14]

Other motives, such as the high estimation of virginity, praised by Christ and his apostle Paul, and the example of monasticism undoubtedly collaborated in creating celibacy regulations. Individual provincial councils like the Council of Toledo in 633, might also have already required a *professio castitatis* from priests in accordance

14. See R. Kottje, "Das Aufkommen der täglichen Eucharistiefeier in der Westkirche und die Zölibatsgesetzgebung," in: *Zeitschrift für Kirchengeschichte* 82 (1971) 218–28, esp. 219: The fourth century was of opinion that "marital intercourse is incompatible with service at the altar."

with monastic example.[15] Yet the laws given general force, particulary the decisive law of Lateran II of 1139, neither take a previous promise by the priest or candidate into consideration, nor are any motives besides purity allowed to surface as grounds for the legal command not to marry.[16]

Only the laws enacted for the entire Roman Catholic Church, such as that of Lateran II, which are to be interpreted in accordance with their wording (see can. 18 CIC), not the decrees of provincial councils, are indeed juridically relevant. Only they represent valid law, not the personal motives of individuals affected by the law – or in reality affected by the charism of celibacy. This is why it seems justified to restrict this study to the decisive laws of the universal Church.

This book's argument can be summarized in two sentences: 1. A gift is necessary for celibacy; this is not given to all priests and without it celibacy leads to illness; 2. The law on celibacy, on the other hand, has taken its origin from the interest in the cultic purity of Old Testament priests, which nowadays is no longer recognized as a sound reason.

The question arising from these two sentences, therefore, runs as follows: Can the law be given a fresh basis by the statement that the requisite charism can be obtained from God by prayer? This is the Vatican Council's answer. Or, if this solution proves to be unworkable, must the law, together with the invalid justification, be seen as untenable?

---

15. E. Schillebeeckx, *Der Amtszölibat. Eine kritische Besinnung* (Theologische Perspektiven, Düsseldorf, 1967) p.50.
16. Cf. Conciliorum Oecumenicorum Decreta (Bologna, 3rd. ed. 1973) p.198. Denzler I, pp.83–5.

Chapter 1

Can the Spiritual Gift of Celibacy be obtained by Prayer?

To solve this question, some New Testament scholarship is indispensable. We must be attentive to revelation. There is a statement in the Gospel of St Matthew, words of the Lord claimed by both supporters and opponents of the law of celibacy: "Not all men can grasp this [not marrying] but only those to whom it has been given. For there are those unable to marry [literally, 'eunuchs'] who have been born as such from their mother's womb; and there are those who have been made eunuchs by men; and there are those unable to marry who have made themselves eunuchs for the sake of the kingdom of heaven. He who is able to grasp this, let him grasp it" (Matt. 19:11f).

We can put to one side the questions of whether this saying of Jesus belongs in his pre-Easter preaching,[1] its relevance within the Matthean redaction[2] and its Old Testament background, since for the purpose of our problem we are concerned only with the actual text, which in its final version is regarded by the Catholic

---

1. Cf. J. Blinzler, *Eisìn eunouchoi. Zur Auslegung von Matt. 19:12*, in *Zeitschrift für die neutestamentliche Wissenschaft* (ZNW) 48 (1957), pp.254–70, here 268f, 265 n.40; H. Baltensweiler, *Die Ehe im Neuen Testament* (Zürich-Stuttgart, 1967) pp.102–12; K. Niederwimmer, *Askese und Mysterium*, (Göttingen, 1975) pp.54–8.
2. J. Dupont, *Mariage et divorce dans l'Evangile* (Bruges, 1959) esp. pp.219–22.

Church as revelation and the word of God.[3] We ask only what this text says as to the possibility of prayer for the spiritual gift to remain unmarried.

1. In the final version of Matthew's Gospel the Lord's saying gives the impression that it should be understood in its immediate context. The disciples' shocked reaction to Jesus' stern pronouncement which allows no divorce save in the case of adultery (19:3–9), was: "If that is the position between husband and wife it is better not to marry" (19:10). Even if this sentence were written as a link-passage[4] by the evangelist, it serves his purpose of connecting the Lord's words about the *eunuchía* in 19:11f with his earlier saying about divorce in 19:8f. Faced with the virtually absolute indissolubility of marriage, the very down-to-earth disciples conclude that it is not good to marry at all. It is to their resigned statement that Jesus' words refer: "Not all men can grasp this [can make this real] but only those to whom it has been given" (19:11): *Ou pántes choroûsin tòn lógon toûton, all' hois dédotai.*

a. All depends on how we should translate the individual words of this statement. It is clearly connected to v.10 by "this" – *toûton* – which refers back to a previous topic as in Matt. 19:22. With regard to the preceding comment of the disciples: better not marry, it must be noticed firstly, that Jesus wants to issue a warning: "Not all" – of you and all men – can do this. The limitation "not all" is emphatically put at the beginning. "Not all men are capable of making this real".

---

3. DS 1501, 3006; Vatican II, *Dei verbum*, in Abbott, p.119.
4. Blinzler, p.267; Dupont, pp.175f; J. Schmid, *Das Evangelium nach Matthäus (Regensburger Neues Testament [RNT], vol. I)* (Regensburg, 4th ed. 1959) p.280.

What does "this" really mean? It has to be the disciples' thoughts on not marrying. This presumption can be affirmed with certainty. M.-J. Lagrange has remarked[5] that *tòn lógon toûton* can mean neither the "word" of Jesus (v.8f) that divorce is the same as adultery, nor the "word" of the disciples given as an answer (v.10), for both words were intended to be understood. The reference must be to something other than words, in fact to some subject. But what? Not the *aitía*, the "situation between husband and wife", because the disciples had understood this "subject" well. Rather it is apparently a new matter which is suggested in the statement by the disciples, namely that one should make up one's mind not to marry. This must be what the Lord means by "this" subject, *tòn lógon toûton*. And in fact *lógos* does not only mean a word, but taken in a Hebrew context it can mean "subject" as well. J. Schmid[6] and M.-J. Lagrange[7] suggest, without giving any special reason, that it can be translated as "this subject". The reason is to be found in the fact that Jesus spoke Aramaic, which is known from the scattering of basic aramaicisms in the Gospels such as *talitha kumi, lama sabachthani, Kephas* and others. Accordingly, the Lords' saying in Matthew 19:11 can be translated back into Aramaic, which is very similar to Hebrew. In both languages, what corresponds to "word" (that is Greek *lógos*) can mean both "word" *and* "subject": the Hebrew *dabar* and the Aramaic *debirah* both have this dual meaning.[8] So, if in our case the meaning

---

5. M.-J. Lagrange, *Evangile selon Matthieu* (Etudes bibliques) (Paris, 8th ed. 1948) p.371.
6. Schmid, pp.279ff.
7. Lagrange, *loc. cit.*: "Rather it is a variant of *aitía*, this thing."
8. On *dabar* see W. Genesius, *Hebräisches und Aramäisches Handwörterbuch über das Alte Testament* (Leipzig, 1915; reprint, 1959).

"word" cannot be considered, then "thing" or "subject" must be intended.

b. "Not all men are capable of making this thing real", namely of voluntarily not marrying. The subject which is not easy to grasp for all men seems clear now. But what is meant by "grasp"? If it does not refer to a "word" it must entail something other than intellectual grasp. Once we have found support by translating the saying back into Aramaic, we should follow this path: What are the equivalents of the Greek word for grasp, *chorein*, in Hebrew? The Hatch-Redpath Concordance shows: in the whole Old Testament there is not a single instance where *chorein* is equivalent to "understand" or "comprehend" or "see". All Hebrew and Aramaic parallels cited in the Concordance to the Septuagint (the Old Testament in Greek)[9] have a spatial reference signifying a "containing" of such and such an amount of something, in one word a spatial capacity. Examples are: "So the land was not big enough [it did not contain both Jakob and Esau] for them to be able to stay together" (Gen. 13:6); "each jug contained 50 *bath*", a measure of water (3 Kings 7:38); "the brazen sea in front of the temple contained 3000 bath" (2 Chr. 4:5). The remaining occurrences of the word *chorein* in the Septuagint: Wisdom 7:23; 2 Maccabees 3:40; 13:26; 15:37, do not correspond with the Hebrew because they are originally written in Greek as were all the late Old Testament writings. However, these texts have just as little to do with "understanding" as the previously cited texts.

It is essential to see the difference between "under-

---

9. E. Hatch and H. Pedpath, *Concordance to the Septuagint*, vol II (Oxford, 1897) 1482.

standing" celibacy and "being capable of it". If the latter is what Christ says "not all" have, then celibacy does not depend on intellectual forces or good will, but on a capacity that is given by God. So, let us try to check whether our findings are reliable: In those cases where the Hebrew words given as parallels for the Greek *chorein* occur independently of Greek parallels, they likewise never mean "to understand", as the Hebrew lexicon says,[10] and the same is true in Aramaic. The words given as parallels in Hatch-Redpath mean, according to the Hebrew lexicon: tie up (*hazaq*), can, be able, contain (*jakal*), measure, measure off (*kul*), lift, carry, suffer (*nasa'*), sleep in a house (*kebet*, from *bajit*, house or container).

A similar result is reached with the Greek word *chorein* itself. According to the dictionaries[11] the root meaning is "to give space", "make room for". Others are: to include, to contain, to collect, especially of an amount. Only once in classical Greek it is found to mean: "take up a thought", a *phrónema*, in Plutarch, *Cato Minor* 4:6. The same applies in New Testament Greek: during the wedding of Cana Christ uses the big jugs of water, "each of which contained from two to three measures" (John 2:6). At the end of his Gospel, John says: "The world would not contain the books that could be written" (John 21:25). And in John 8:37 Christ states with regard to the Jews in front of him: "My word does not find any place in you, you act like your father, the devil", which means

---

10. See Gesenius on *hazaq, jakal, kul, nasa'* and *kebet*.
11. H.G. Liddell and R. Scott, *A Greek-English Lexicon* (Oxford, 9th ed. 1966) 2015; W. Bauer, *Griechisch-Deutsches Handwörterbuch zu den Schriften des Neues Tetaments* (Berlin, 5th ed. 1958) 1758.

that *chorein* has something to do with action, not with understanding.[12]

Bauer's dictionary says[13] that there is only one instance "of the intellectual sense: receive, understand", and he points to Matthew 19:11, our verse. But this would be a dangerous supposition because it would be a vicious circle to interpret Matthew 19:11 in isolation: if there is no other instance of an "intellectual" meaning, it is not sound to take this meaning for granted. Rather we should apply the spatial connotation which is always preferred in the New Testament: "This subject of not marrying does not find place in all men".

We are led to the conclusion that in all Hebrew and Aramaic, and in almost all Greek occurrences of the word *chorein* or equivalents the meaning to be given to it is spatial, bodily, one might almost say physical, and not that of comprehension. So too in Matthew 19:11 this meaning will have to be applied: "grasp" in this verse does not refer to acceptance with the mind, because it does not refer back to a word but to a newly introduced subject, that is the possible advantage of not marrying (Matt. 19:10). Its sense is: "Not all men have space in themselves, are capable of making real this matter [voluntarily refraining from marriage]". A "matter" must be "done" – a "word" must be "understood". The physical meaning of *lógos* as "matter" is supported by the physical meaning of *chorein* as to "realize" celibacy.

A last check: there are enough Greek words specifically meaning "to understand with the mind": *gnõnai*, *syniénai*, *noeîn*, as well as in Hebrew and Aramaic *jada'*.

---

12. Liddell-Scott also places Matt. 19:11f, the verse we are examining, here, in comparison with John 8:37.
13. Bauer, 1759.

This result must be pondered in view of the limitation "not all men" which was remarked at the outset. It is now becoming clearer which group of people the Lord was actually thinking of in the phrase "Not all men can grasp this": only those who in body and soul, in their psycho-physical being have an ability to accept celibacy. To repeat: according to Jesus's words, what has not been given to everyone is not the intellectual ability to understand the thought of a celibate life, but the personal psychological and bodily ability to live it. The one who cannot live it does not lack understanding of celibacy for the sake of the kingdom of heaven. Celibacy does not depend on aims and good intentions in the individual, rather it depends on a psycho-physical ability which one either has or does not have.

c. This most important piece of information is fully obtained from the second part of the phrase: not all can grasp this (the ability not to marry) "but only those to whom it has ben given" (Matthew 19:11b); the Greek is *all' hoîs dédotai*. Jesus here calls the combined power of body and soul to grasp celibacy a "gift" of God's special grace. It was his way of speaking to express God's activity through the passive voice:[14] "it has been given to them". From this wording we learn that celibacy is a gift from God, not shared by all, a charism.

This means, I cannot achieve it through my own powers. Therefore Jesus issues the warning and gives the reason for it: be aware, not everyone is capable of celibacy, since a special divine gift of grace is needed. We are forced to infer: woe betide anyone who tries without

---

14. So called *passivum divinum*. Cf. J. Jeremias, *Die Abendmahlsworte Jesu* (Göttingen, 4th ed. 1966) p.194f; Blinzler, p.265. Eng. trans. *The Eucharistic Words of Jesus*. London and New York, 1966.

such a special gift of God's grace, since it was God himself who said: "It is not good for the human being to be alone" (Gen. 2:18).

This implies that those who have not received the gift of celibacy are psycho-physically incapable, unable to live in this state of life. They are not disposed to celibate life by grace, so will place undue stress on themselves by attempting it nonetheless. There is an incapacity in them which, if ignored, would lead to neurosis. Paul calls this incapacity *akrasía*, an inability to abstain from marriage (1 Cor. 7:5). In this case he advises marriage.

A final observation on the last word of v.11 is decisive for our problem of praying for this gift: it is put in the perfect tense: *dédotai*, it has been given (beforehand). This tense clearly shows that the granting of the gift of God's grace has already happened in the past of those concerned, not in their future. Either they received it in the past, if not in the cradle, or they do not have it at all. With this information the question seems to be settled whether the charism of celibacy can be prayed for or not. Jesus says openly: "Not all men can grasp this [present] but only those to whom it has been given [perfect]". If the sequence of tenses applies, then the "given" must precede the ability to "grasp". Had Jesus wanted to say that the gift of grace can be asked for, a future would have had to follow the present tense, something like: "Only those can grasp it to whom it will be given". There are instances of this way of speaking and such invitation to prayer: James invites his readers to pray for wisdom. "If any of you lacks wisdom let him ask for it, and it will be given to him [*dothésetai*, future]" (James 1:5). Likewise in Matthew 19:11 only the future would have constituted an invitation to prayer. If Christ uses the perfect tense, he makes clear that the gift of celibacy is not obtainable by prayer, a fact which he confirms in the following verse 19:12. The charism is a supernatural talent, akin to a musical talent which can be furthered or wasted but is not at the disposition of a person. Of course, the one who is called can and must pray that he recognize the gift and nurture it, but he cannot successfully pray for the gift as such.

d. We can now turn to Matthew 19:12. It contains the reason for v.11 because it is introduced with the word "for", which links it to the preceding verse. The core of Jesus' teaching about celibacy is already found in v.11. The next verse gives an explanation. That is why Vatican II adduces Matthew 19:11 alone as support for calling celibacy a high gift from God.[15] Verse 12 illustrates what Jesus meant, by a comparison. It confirms our findings: "For there are eunuchs who have been born as such from their mother's womb; and there are those who have been made eunuchs by men; and there are those who have made themselves eunuchs for the sake of the kingdom of heaven. He who is able to grasp this, let him grasp it".

Anyone can observe the exact correspondence of tenses: just as the perfect tense in v.11 describes a given situation – "it *has been* given to them" –, so we have here the present tense doing the same – describing that "there *are* some unable to marry" -, and the triple times past tense (aorist) which describes past situations: Some have been born as such, some have been made so by men, some have made themselves eunuchs, by the power of the antecedent gift from God. Nothing can be done about those who are impotent or have been castrated. In fact, the "eunuch" saying of Jesus does suggest that there is a

---

15. PO 16f, note 194, Abbott, p. 566.

parallel between charismatic voluntary celibacy and the
enforced kind due to physical(!) incapacity. Just as the
first two examples in Jesus' *mashal* – a wise saying – are
taken from man's physical body, so also the God-given
capacity for celibacy expresses itself through a bodily,
that is to say an all-embracing capability. A *mashal*,
though, is no allegory in which the individual elements
may be exploited,[16] yet if there is to be any sense in
bringing together the three classes of eunuchs in one
saying, it must be because there are parallels between
them. All three are eunuchs, "castrated", only the way
they have become so is different. Dupont[17] points out
that this difference is implicit in the stylistic form of a
mashal: eunuchs are mentioned three times but the point
of a wise saying is always that the third element must be
taken in a wholly different sense. That, of course,
remains true even if the similarity of the three eunuchs
cannot be overlooked. Because of the *parallelismus
membrorum*, the similarity must almost necessarily be
kept precisely in a wise saying since it lifts the term up to
a superior level at the end[18]. We can see the scale: the
inability to marry in the impotent exists from the cradle,
is "given" as a *datum* of their life; *castrati*, as well, have to
respect the fact of their mutilation, usually done against
their will; but it is otherwise, though similar, with the
eunuchs for the sake of the kingdom of heaven: they
have also already been given the ability to live unmarried but this is due to grace and not to the way they
were created or made by man. Apart from this, they are

---

16. Cf. the famous work by A. Jülicher, *Die Gleichnisreden Jesu*, vol.I
(Tübingen, 2nd ed. 1910), p.70; Dupont, p.197.
17. Dupont, p.197.
18. So called "climax", cf. F. Nötscher, *Die Psalmen* (Echterbibel, vol.4,
Würzburg, 2nd ed. 1959), p.11.

free to accept and to realize this gift, or possibly even not to, since it follows: "they have made themselves unable to marry for the sake of the kingdom of heaven".

Hence "eunuch" must be taken, if not in a literal sense (as Origen did), at least in a realistic one. Some of those taken over by the kingdom of God are spiritually unable to marry. "For the sake of the kingdom" means the motivation of their free will, but their *eunuchía* is in the same way impossible without the grace of God, just as the *eunuchía* of the two first examples is impossible without the interference of God as creator in the first instance or of men in the second. If verse 12 is to prove verse 11, since it is introduced by "for there are [other] eunuchs", then Jesus by verse 12 seeks to demonstrate the small number of spiritual eunuchs or those capable of celibacy as well as the God-given character of their capability. No one can stay unmarried for the kingdom of heaven unless he has been prepared for it.

e. The foregoing shows clearly the relation between the bodily "inability to marry" (*eunuchía*) in verse 12 and the bodily, psycho-physical "ability not to marry" in verse 11. He who can "grasp" celibacy is similar to a "eunuch" who is unable to marry. How closely the verses 11 and 12 are woven together – it seems by Jesus himself, not only by Matthew – can be deduced from the repetition of "grasp" at the end of verse 12: "He who is able to grasp it, let him grasp it", in Greek: *hò dynámenos choreîn choreîto*.

With the words "who is able" (*dynámenos*), the "to whom it is given" of verse 11 is taken up again, and "grasp" is repeated literally. Apparently Jesus does not invite prayer for the gift, but he admonishes the individual to recognize and accept the gift which is already given to him and which Jesus presupposes: who can shall grasp. Not those who cannot grasp. And not those who wish to grasp. He who feels that he can shall follow the invitation of God to a lifestyle for which God's antecedent grace has given him the strength. That is all Jesus is saying here. It may be summarized like this: "Be aware of wishing rather to stay unmarried! There are only a few capable of that. Some physically impotent may easily do it, and some spiritually endowed by God can do it for the sake of the kingdom of heaven. If you don't belong to one of these small groups, hands off, content yourself with the gift of marriage!"[19]

2. Very similar ideas are expressed in a saying of Paul (1 Cor. 7:7). Paul agrees with Jesus in the high estimation given to the celibate life as a charism. He invents this word for the "gift" from God, especially in connection with celibacy and marriage. Moreover, he remarks on nearly unsurmountable barriers between both charisms, as well as the fact that "not all" are capable of celibacy.

He states his preference for celibacy in the words: "I would that all men were indeed as I am. However, each has his special spiritual gift [*chárisma*] from God, one of this kind, one of another." In view of the soon expected return of the Lord,[20] Paul would wish everyone to be

19. Quentin Quesnel's article: "Made themselves eunuchs for the Kingdom of Heaven (Matt. 19:12)", in: *Catholic Biblical Quarterly* 30 (1968), pp.335–58, suffers from the misinterpretation of *chorein* as "understanding". In his eyes, Jesus' injunction not to divorce as explained in the preceding pericope Matt. 19:6–9, is "a mystery, the understanding of which is given only to a few" (Quesnel, p.349). The main objection to be made against his position is: *Eunuchía* means literally impossibility to marry at all, not fidelity to a first and unique marriage. Besides, fidelity in marriage is one of the Ten Commandements for all, while in fact celibacy is a gift only for a few.
20. Cf. 1 Cor. 7:26–31.

unmarried like him. Yet he, like the Lord, adds a warning with the stressed "However" (*allà*, not just *dè*): for this state of life there is need of a special grace from God. Obviously his wish to see all Christians unmarried is unfulfillable because God gives different graces: one person has the gift of celibacy while another has the gift of marriage. Both then are spiritual gifts, "gifts from God", as *chárisma* is here explained. In this respect both have the same value before God and man. Yet they are different and, it seems, not exchangeable. The recipient of one gift cannot, obviously, be the beneficiary of the other, even if he would wish so, otherwise Paul's desire that he might see everyone remaining unmarried could be fulfilled!

Here too, it is decisive for our question to pay attention to the tense: *échei*, each one "has" his own gift from God. The present tense describes a state, as does the perfect tense in the Lord's saying: it "has been given to them" (Matt. 19:11). This appears to be an unchangeable state, a distinguishing feature of everyone. It cannot be removed, not even by the wish of a high church authority, such as the apostle Paul. And this difference among human beings is represented by Paul as being quite unaffected by the imminent second coming of the Lord: it is simply dependent on God's different ways of spreading his grace. Thus Paul refrains himself from praying or inviting prayer for the charism of celibacy. This is not by chance; if it were possible to pray for this gift, he would have encouraged this in the same way as he does in the case of other charisms. With regard to love he says: "Seek the higher spiritual gifts, especially the one of love" (1 Cor. 12:31). This is a way for all. Celibacy, on the contrary, is not for all because not everyone has been 'given' it, as the Lord himself says in Matthew

19:11. Paul picks it up with the wording *ídion chárisma*, each has his own, or special, "gift" (1 Cor. 7:7). It is clear, then, according to Paul, that one cannot "seek" the gift of celibacy as one can "seek" love. One cannot pray for it. Paul says either a man "has" it, or he does not have it; in the latter case, instead, he "has" the gift or ability to marry. Both are gifts already granted by God and can only be accepted and developed. Prayer would not change anything in the nature and presence of the different gifts. It could only aim at perseverance in the gift. – Only later on, after the maturing experience of marriage, can widowhood possibly take its place.[21]

---

21. The status of widowhood is attested by Paul: 1 Cor. 7:8; 1 Tim. 5:3–16. Paul does not admit younger widows to be accepted, which shows that he respects nature.

Chapter 2

Consequences for the Law on Celibacy

The findings of exegesis, that is the data of revelation, provide the criteria by which we should assess the history of the later law on celibacy and the grounds for its present-day validity.

The Introduction showed that the church order not to marry has been broken at all times and in many ways. If we compare this fact with the results of exegesis, must we not reach the conclusion that this law could not be kept by all just because the Lord said: "Not all men are capable of making this state of life real, but only those to whom it has been given by God"? No law-giver prior to the Council of Trent considered these words of the Lord: and Trent did so only by way of allusion (*en passant*). They were given greater consideration by the Second Vatican Council. Yet the only possible (though very doubtful) justification for this law would have lain in reliance on the above saying of Jesus and in the Church's express wish to accept for the priestly office only those candidates who have received the gift of celibacy from God.

This demand suggested by the data of revelation was neither satisfied during the law's early history, nor in the renewed injunction by the Second Vatican Council, although it intended to make statements along these lines. Rather, both morally misunderstood cultic require-

ments of the Old Testament and Hellenistic ideas of a
suggested incompatibility between sexuality and
priestly service were at work. These led not to a principle
of selection for admission to priesthood, but to the
demand for restraint within a valid Christian marriage.
This was already the case in Elvira in Spain (around 303
or 324), under Popes Damasus and Siricius (385) and all
succeeding Popes. The demand next led to priestly
marriage being forbidden altogether and declared null at
the Second Lateran Council (1139) and again in the
Codex Iuris Canonici (1918). It was indeed the Second
Vatican Council that for the first time expressly brought
into its discussions the charism which is required for
restraint on religious grounds, yet it did not draw any
conclusions from this with regard to the law. Neither did
do so the New Code of 1983 which simply repeated the
"obligation of continence", the *"obligatio* to celibacy",
calling it abruptly "a special gift from God" without
making any attempt to reconcile the notions of gift and
obligation (can. 277 § 1).

Both these statements, about the misunderstood Old
Testament motivation for the law as well as about the
absence of the notion of charism before Vatican II, need
to be proven. Suffice it to spotlight the decisive turning-
points of the legislation, since what had earlier been
decreed was only repeated. The decisive phases are the
beginning and the end of the legislation, namely the
fourth and the twelfth centuries.

1. In the fourth century, the provincial council of the
Spanish bishops in Elvira was the first – according to the
view prevailing to the present – which forbade priests of
higher rank to continue their marriage after ordination.
Its canon 33 declares: "It was decided to forbid all

serving clergy: they are to keep themselves from their wives and are not to produce any children".[1]

M. Meigne has recently demonstrated in a comparative study[2] the important reasons for dating by far the greater part of the 81 canons of Elvira (namely, canons 22–62 and 76–81) as originating from a later time and being added to the 21 of the synod of 303 to form a collection. Canon 33, in particular, presents a summary form of an oriental Church canon, namely can. 51 of the so-called Apostolic Canons dating from 380 or 400. If we read Canon 33 in the light of this original context, it says just the opposite to what has been understood by it until now. It is, in fact, to be taken literally in its double negation: "It was decided to forbid keeping back from one's wife and not producing children", just as canon 51 of the Apostolic Canons forbids "refraining from marriage, from meat and from wine, insofar as this is done out of contempt, not out of asceticism, as blasphemy against the creator", and excommunicates the clergy in question.[3]

---

1. DS 118 (D 52c). The period 300–303 is generally regarded as the date of the council, cf. DS 117 (D 52a); according to Denzler I,7 it took place "presumably not before 324", but a still later date has probably to be supposed for the canon 33 in question, cf. next footnote. The text runs in the original Latin: *"Placuit in totum prohibere episcopis, presbyteris et diaconibus, vel omnibus clericis positis in ministerio, abstinere se a coniugibus suis et non generare filios; quicumque vero fecerit, ab honore clericatus exterminetur".*

2. M. Meigne, "Concile ou Collection d'Elvire?" in: *Revue d'Histoire Ecclésiastique* 70 (1975), pp.361–87. I have to thank Herr H.U. Wili, author of the article: "Zur Zölibatspflicht der Weltkleriker im katholischen Kirchenrecht" (*Theologische Berichte* 4, Cologne-Einsiedeln-Zürich, 1974), pp.183–244, for drawing my attention to the article by Meigne, and also for numerous points of canon law and suggested correction.

3. See F. X. Funk, *Didaskalia et Constitutiones Apostolorum* (Paderborn, 1905), p.581: *"Si quis episcopus aut presbyter aut diaconus aut quilibet e*

Were canon 33 of Elvira to be understood in this way, then here, once more, western canon law would be in agreement with eastern canon law and its apostolic origins (cf. 1 Tim 3:2 and 4:1–5).

However, the North African Council of Carthage in 401 expressed itself in a manner similar to Elvira in the former interpretation, and Spain and Italy too towards the end of the fourth century actually promulgated laws with the explicit intention of forbidding priests any marital cohabitation, as can be seen from the letter of Pope Siricius dated 10 February 385 to Bishop Himerius of Tarragona in Spain.[4] Pope Siricius in his letter

---

numero clericorum nuptiis et carnibus et vino se abstinet, non propter exercitationem, sed propter detestationem, oblitus quod 'omnia valde bona' et quod 'masculum et feminam fecit Deus hominem', sed blasphemans accusat creationem, aut corrigatur aut deponatur et ex ecclesia eiciatur; similiter et laicus", quoted by Meigne, p.382.

4. Fifth Council of Carthage of 401: cf. *Decretum Gratiani* d.32 c.13 (ed. Friedberg I, 120f; no. 163 for dating information): *"Placuit episcopos, presbiteros, diaconos, secundum priora instituta etiam abstinere ab uxoribus; quod nisi fecerint, ab ecclesiastico removeantur officio"*. The *Letter of Pope Siricius* is extensively reproduced in Denzinger up to the 32nd edition (D 89), since then in a shortened form in DS 185 (D 183 for dating information: 10 Feb. 385). The most important passages read: *"Plurimos enim sacerdotes Christi atque levitas, post longa consecrationis suae tempora, tam de coniugiis propriis, quam etiam de turpi coitu sobolem didicimus procreasse, et crimen suum hac praescriptione defendi, quia in Veteri Testamento sacerdotibus... generandi facultas legitur attributa... Cur (Dominus) eos... praemonet dicens: Sancti estote, quia ego sanctus sum Dominus Deus vester?... Omnes sacerdotes atque levitas insolubili lege constringimur, ut a die ordinationis nostrae pudicitiae et corda nostra mancipemus et corpora. Ii vero, qui... excusatione nituntur, noverint se ab omni ecclesiastico honore deiectos nec umquam posse veneranda attrectare mysteria, quibus se ipsi, dum obscoenibus cupiditatibus inhiant, privaverunt"*. Compare, in contrast to this western legislation, the virtually contemporary eastern legislation in the 51st "Apostolic Canon" (dated 380–400), see note 3. Meigne has convincingly shown that these eastern canons affected the Latin collections of the fourth century, so they were known in the west. *Apostolic Canon 51 refers to*

complains "that very many priests, long after their ordination, have produced offspring with their own wives", which he equates with unchastity (*turpi coitu*) and calls a crime (*crimen*). The letter presents an unrelieved diatribe against the duties of marriage as being an "unholy" matter: only total abstinence would raise the clergy to the holiness required by God. Support for this opinion is sought in Lev. 20:7, a passage that in fact deals with the people of Israel as a whole, not only priests; and this people, as is well known, placed a very high value on marriage precisely because of the promises concerning its descendant, the Messiah. The lowest point of the argument in the letter is reached when it calls the reproductive act – even within Christian marriage – a "pursuit after obscene lusts". Here, a quite general "horror" is expressed about sexuality as a whole.

In view of 1 Thessalonians 4:4; Hebrews 13:4; 1 Peter 3:7 and Ephesians 5:23–32 – these being the most important biblical assertions that holiness in marriage is possible – the judgment of Pope Siricius on the reproductive act can only be designated a mistake. According to the criteria which, at least nowadays, are laid down for a law to be just and to have binding force, the fourth century law shows itself to be a *lex iniqua*. A law has to be "morally good" with respect to the "content" and the "purpose", say Mörsdorf and Häring.[5] Both the criteria seem to be "bad" in the law in

---

the order of creation; this demonstrates that the difference was apparent between "natural law" and purely "human law"; see the term of "natural law" already in classical Roman legislation, as Ulpian (220–230) formulates it *Digesta* I,1,1,3: *"Ius naturale est, quod natura omnia animalia docuit"*. Therefore, the clash with revelation and the injustice of the abstinence laws, was understandable to the fourth century lawgivers, on the basis of contemporary criteria.

5. See above, Introduction, note 10.

question: Both the *reason* for not allowing priests to procreate – namely that sexual union in marriage is obscene – and the *purpose* – to keep priests unsullied by "protecting them from" this obscene activity – are morally wrong, because they involve a general disparagement of marriage. Consequently the purpose removes from the law its binding force, at least in current estimation. The *content*, the subject matter of the law, also goes against the teaching of revelation, against the commandment of the "Lord", that "the wife should not separate from her husband" (1 Cor 7:10), and that of the Apostle Paul: "Do not refuse one another except perhaps by agreement for a season, but then come together again, lest Satan tempt you through lack of self-control" (1 Cor 7:5). Since these sentences were known to the fourth century legislators, they had the means to appreciate the moral wrongfulness of their law, insofar as it took away from priests the rights and duties of marriage. With that, the original celibacy regulation is proved – even by the standards of contemporary history – to be vitiated both in its purpose and content, as contradicting revelation and the divine law.

In any case, present-day canon law teaching has to regard the fourth century law as void, since the Codex Iuris Canonici regards "the conjugal act which by itself is apt to produce offspring' (*coniugalis actus per se aptus ad prolis generationem*), as belonging to the enduring 'essence of marriage' (*ad quem natura sua ordinatur matrimonium*), which is guaranteed by 'divine law' and in consequence, cannot be removed by the ecclesiastical lawgiver (canons 1061 §1; 1057 §2; 1059, CIC/1983).

If the celibacy law has arisen from such murky sources, it cannot have been justified solely by its long existence. Interestingly enough, this justification has often been tried right up to the present. Denzler names a whole series of popes and synods who rely on the "ancient canons".[6] On the other hand, the non-ecumenical Eastern Trullum Synod of 692 refers to the still older *apostolic* law; possibly 1 Timothy 3:2, Titus 1:6 and the "Apostolic Canons" may be meant: "Since we have learnt that in the Church of the Romans it is handed down as a law that deacons and priests have to promise restraint from intercourse with their wives, we wish, following the old law observed and prescribed by the apostles, that the legal marriages of ordained men shall continue to be valid (*sacrorum virorum legales nuptias amodo valere volumus*) in that we in no way put an end to their cohabitation. They shall not be forced (*cogantur!*) to promise at the time of their ordination that they would have to restrain themselves... He who takes upon himself, contrary to the apostolic canons, to stop priests and deacons from having relations and fellowship with their legal wives is to be removed from office". This massive criticism from the East has found a place in Gratian's *Decretum* of 1142.[7] So it was certainly known in the West and the later Latin legislators of all times could have been aware of the contradiction between their tradition and the original, apostolic tradition.

Yet, even Pope Paul VI, in his encyclical *Sacerdotalis caelibatus*, still exploited the thought that it is "unthinkable that the Church followed a path, which...in a certain sense had put at risk...the spiritual wealth of individual souls, throughout the centuries".[8] This shows his awareness that the law may give rise to problems.

---

6. Denzler I and II *passim*, e.g. I,165, 169. See also DS 185, n.1.
7. Gratian, D.31 c.13 (ed. Friedberg I,114).
8. *Sacerdotalis caelibatus* n. 41, in: *Acta Apostolicae Sedis* (AAS) 59 (1967) p.674.

Pope John XXIII also did so. His words in answer to the
French philosopher Etienne Gilson are well known: he
thought he often heard the weeping of young priests
who groan beneath the burden of this law.[9] Yet, so runs
the significant reasoning in favour of retaining the law:
he can, nevertheless, not simply take a pen and repeal it;
for then, how would it still be possible to speak of the
"one holy and chaste church"?

Here again, that basic attitude of hostility to marriage
which dominates the letter of Pope Siricius is clearly
having its effect: is chastity not possible perhaps, within
marriage? From the words of Pope Paul VI quoted in the
Introduction,[10] that priests and religious "care for the
purity of the body", similar tendencies of animosity to
marriage can be deduced. The original motives for the
law are still at work right up to the present. Therefore,
the doubt as to the moral goodness of content and
purpose of the law must be extended to the present day,
as well. We shall see, later on, whether better reasons for
the law have been found by Vatican II.

A recent work on celibacy, the book by R. Cholij,[11]
denies in vain that the western rule of continence was
based upon a rejection of something "impure". C.H.
Lawrence qualified his work as "Unconvincing arguments against a married priesthood": "In the absence of
historical evidence for such observance (that from the
Apostolic age onwards priests were required to abstain
from conjugal relations after ordination), the author

---

9. Denzler II,415f. Pope Paul VI too quoted his predecessor in
Sacerdotalis caelibatus n. 37: AAS 59 (1967), p.672: The Church is unable
to annul the celibacy law, *"nam hoc est insigne victoriae Ecclesiae
Christi..., ut sit libera, casta, universalis"*.
10. See Introduction note 8.
11. R. Cholij, *Clerical celibacy in East and West* (Leominster, 1989).

appeals to the almost universal consensus of the early councils prohibiting *marriage* after ordination".[12] In fact, abstinence *in* marriage was required only from the times of Siricius onwards, and, as has been shown, for the reason of "impurity" of conjugal acts – against the massive criticism of the Eastern Church.

2. In the second decisive phase of the law's development in the twelfth century the blemish of its illegitimate birth still attached to celibacy as a law. The Second Lateran Council of 1139 in its seventh canon alleges only one thing, other than enjoining an "ancient law", as the purpose for declaring void marriages contracted by priests after their ordination: "so that the *purity* pleasing to God may be spread among those belonging to the Church and those who are ordained" (*ut lex continentiae et deo placens munditia in ecclesiasticis personis et sacris ordinibus dilatetur.*)[13] If marriage of priests was forbidden and that already entered was sundered and declared null for the sole purpose that "purity" might be spread, it can only be concluded that the Fathers of the council considered marriage not as pure but as impure – *tertium non datur*. In that, they too are seen to suffer from the delusion apparent from the outset, that self-abandonment within marriage is something impure in principle.[14] Hence, the same applies to the law of 1139 as

---

12. The Tablet, 6 January 1990, p.14.
13. *Conciliorum Oecumenicorum Decreta*, ed. J. Alberigo, P.P. Joannou, C. Leonardi et P. Prodi (Freiburg, 1962) p.175, (Bologna, 3rd ed. 1973) p.198.
14. Cf. M. Müller, *Die Lehre des hl. Augustinus von der Paradiesesehe und ihre Auswirkung in der Sexualethik des 12. und 13. Jahrhunderts bis Thomas v. Aquin* (Regensburg, 1954), esp. p.279: Soon after Augustine the simplified formula, "no conception without sin" appeared.

applied to that of 385: the definition of the *purpose* as being to keep priests from impure deeds within marriage makes the celibacy law of the twelfth century into a law which is not justifiable on moral grounds, and which, from a present-day viewpoint at least, cannot claim any binding legal force.

The same holds true for the *content*, the very matter of the law. It requires "that those, who have had the audacity to marry, are to be separated, because such a union is considered by us. . . not to be a marriage".[15]

Right up to the twelfth century priestly marriages had been regarded as forbidden, but not as null and void. Now, without taking account of the freedom of choice of those affected, the council interfered with priests' natural right to marry and took it away from them completely. Still more: priestly marriages already entered into and which, up to that point, were held to be valid, were "dissolved" and with that marriage bonds which continued in the sight of God were loosened, against Matthew 19:6: ". . .let no man put asunder". Both were impossibilities according to legal understanding in former times and also at the present time because the right to marry is a divine and natural right (Gen 1:28; 2:18, 24) (more on this below in Chapter 4) and because marriage once validly contracted is indissoluble. At most, according to earlier understanding as well, a law *ex tunc* could have decided the nullity of future marriages (cf. can. 9 CIC) – if that were possible. According to biblical teaching on marriage and celibacy (which did not, however, enter into the Lateran Council's consideration at all), such a law too is to be regarded as going against revelation, since it infringes a divine right and attempts

---

15. Conc. Oec. Decr. (see note 13), p.175 (198).

to impose something which is impossible without a spiritual gift from God.

This law has to be regarded as null, not only from a present-day viewpoint, but also by contemporary standards. The council Fathers were conscious that they were pronouncing only a church rule, an *"ecclesiastica regula"*, which is unable to annul a divine right; and as to the purpose of the law, they were aware of the holiness of marriage, since they themselves, for the first time, defined the sacramental nature of marriage: "Those who condemn the sacraments. . .and the legitimate bonds of marriage – we condemn them as heretics [*Eos qui. . . sacramentum. . . et legitimarum damnant foedera nuptiarum, tanquam haereticos damnamus*]".[16] Hence canon 7 of the Second Lateran Council in 1139 is a *lex iniqua* which, even in those days, could not claim any validity because the legislation of the Council went against its own teaching. It is not possible with a clear conscience to emphasize at the same time the sacramental rank of marriage and to forbid priests the marital act on the grounds that it is "impure".

3. The Council of Trent did not promulgate any new law but only confirmed the old one within the canons on marriage (!), in the form of the marital obstacle of ordination. Here, the council mentioned the "gift of chastity", the *donum castitatis*, for the first time, though, it must be said, not in a statement of its own but in a quotation from the Reformers. The council simply sought to reject their position without deep discussion of the issue. In canon 9 of the twenty-fourth session in 1563,

---

16. DS 718. Cf. also below, the distinction between *"sancimus"* in Pisa 1123 and *"censemus"* (which is less strong) in Lateran II of 1139, chapter 4, nn. 18f.

the opinion that "all clerics and members of religious orders who realize that they do not have the gift of chastity, could marry"[17] is rejected. It is the general opinion of theologians that, here, we do not have a comprehensive view of the charism, but, according to the council's declared intent, only the condemnation of the teaching of the Reformers, "which throws doubt on the competence of Church authority (concerning marriage)".[18] All the same, the council saw itself forced to enter into the Reformers' biblical argument that a charism is required for celibacy, to the extent that in a closing sentence, which is meant to give the grounds for the condemnation, it answers the Reformers: "For to those who ask him aright, God will not refuse the gift".

This brings us to the core of the problem. The Tridentine statement apparently contradicts what the New Testament teaches about the gift of the ability not to marry for the sake of the Kingdom, namely that it is given or not given but cannot be obtained by prayer. Canon 9 of Trent defines solely the existence of the Church's marital obstacle of ordination and of solemn vow. It can be questioned whether, with respect to ordination, this is an item of discipline or morals. Discipline cannot ever be defined "dogmatically". In any case, the post-posited reason for the obstacle is not included in a definition which normally runs as follows: "who says such and such a thing, be he condemned, *anathema sit*". The following reason is in no way included

---

17. DS 1809: *"Si quis dixerit, clericos... posse omnes contrahere matrimonium qui non sentiunt se castitatis... habere donum: an. s."* Cf. Denzler I, 389.
18. Schillebeeckx, (see Intro., n.15) p.35 n.69. Cf. DS 1800.

in the condemnation. Doubt as to this reason, therefore, is not affected by it.[19]

Furthermore, it was no accident that the reason was placed outside the canon. Rather it was done purposely. During the council's last session, which took place under pressure of time,[20] only a few anathems were put into effect: these were to ensure the sacramental worth of marriage – against Luther's *dictum* that marriage was "a worldly thing" – and to form the basis of the Church's competence in matters of marriage. Thus, the Council only incidentally mentioned the *donum castitatis*. Here too the implicit restriction of "chastity" to unmarried persons is striking. This way of speaking is very close to that of Siricius and Lateran II in which purity is achievable only outside of marriage. But our main interest here is in Trent's teaching on celibacy. There is no closer examination of the gift's connection with the priesthood. Priesthood was not even at issue in the canons concerned with marriage. Rather, the existing law was simply to be reinforced anew, as it were, in passing: (*"non obstante lege ecclesiatica vel voto"*) but not given a fresh basis.[21] On the evidence of the council's documents,[22] one lone Father, the Bishop of Lucca, drew attention to the difference between vows of Orders and "a promise of restraint which is connected with divine ordination (*sic*)" (he did not speak of law!). However,

---

19. See above, Intro., end of par.1.
20. Cf. H. Jedin, *Geschichte des Konzils von Trient* IV,2 (Freiburg, 1975), pp.136f.
21. Schillebeeckx, *loc. cit.*: "The Council of Trent has only defended the legitimacy of the practice on this point since the Second Lateran Council".
22. *Concilium Tridentinum, Diariorum, Actorum, Epistularum Tractatuum Nova Collectio* (CT), ed. Societas Goerresiana, tom. IX (Freiburg, 1924), pp.639–968 *passim*.

that interested him only in regard to the difference in the marital obstacles resulting from both "promises".[23] Cardinal Guise of Lorraine, the most powerful man at the council, suggested that a new sentence on the *donum castitatis* (which was not originally intended!) should be inserted into the text: "God will grant this in sufficient measure to all who ask".[24] The Archbishop of Rossano in Calabria replied somewhat later that it was better to add it *after* the *"anathema sit"*, i.e. outside the condemnation,[25] and that is indeed what happened in the final text.[26]

This short history of the canon shows that no discussion on the charism took place. The sentence inserted to defend the law was merely displaced from its place within the canon itself. This happened intentionally. So, it was not meant as part of the definition but represented a fallible opinion of the council Fathers.

We come to the conclusion that the Council of Trent said nothing new on the law of 1139, and did not come to definite terms with the notion of charism first introduced by the Reformers. What was said, therefore, about the canon 7 of Lateran II might also apply to canon 9 of the 24th session of Trent. Trent presupposed an existing law which in fact was null and void, and tried to justify the law by the idea of possibly obtaining the gift of celibacy by prayer. But it did not make a dogma of this idea.

This glance back at the council of Trent provides the

---

23. CT IX, 674, 6–15.
24. CT IX, 687, 11: "Lotharingus: In 9. addatur: *Cum Deus illud det sufficienter omnibus petentibus"*.
25. CT IX, 781, 34.
26. CT IX, 889, 23 and 968, 5: *"...A.S., cum Deus id recte petentibus non deneget"*.

important clarification needed to evaluate the recent treatment of the subject "gift and law of celibacy" at the Second Vatican Council on 7 December 1965. Trent's statement that God gives the charism of celibacy to all who ask aright is no dogma. Thus, there is also no need to attribute the weight of dogma to Vatican II's similar statement .

4. In the Vatican II Decree on *The Ministry and Life of Priests* their celibate state is made the object of discussion by a council in the sort of detail unparalleled up to that moment (PO 16). Nevertheless, the council Fathers have not been able to offer a truly satisfactory solution to the problem.[27]

a. To begin with, it has to be thankfully acknowledged that the council carefully abstained from repeating the "purity" motifs, based on cultus and heathen hostility to the body, when justifying the law. Already the leading term *"perfecta continentia"* (complete continence) finally puts an end to the centuries-long devaluation of marriage which was contained in the term, otherwise always used for unmarried life: *"perfecta castitas"* (complete chastity),[28] since perfect chastity is due and possible in marriage too. Furthermore, the married priests of the Eastern Churches (let it be noted, of the Catholic Eastern Churches united to Rome), are considered worthy of an

---

27. Cf. the commentary by F. Wulf SJ on PO 16 in LThK, 2nd ed., Council III, 214–21. Se also the "Response" by J.O. Nelson, Abbott, pp.577–9.

28. So for example as recently as in Pius XII's encyclical *Sacra virginitas*: AAS 46 (1954), pp.161–191: *"Sacra virginitas et perfecta illa castitas..."*

approving mention,[29] which had still been anxiously avoided at the Council of Trent.[30] The word contained in the draft of the Tridentine canon which demonstrated that the discipline of celibacy was limited to the West was struck out again at the wish of many council Fathers: "Cancel 'western' priests". As a result, the existence of married Catholic priests in the eastern part of the Catholic Church remained largely unknown in the West until today. Even more so, the 1990 Synod of Bishops, dealing with the education of future priests, returned to the practice of Trent and suppressed, "at the last minute", a planned mention of the eastern discipline when praising celibacy: "While the different practice in the eastern churches shall remain safe, celibacy gave a bright light. . .".[31] The first words were cancelled. The motives of the council Fathers of Trent, and of the Synod Fathers of Rome in 1990, are obvious: They did not want to give any foothold to the demand for equality in law in the West. Vatican II on the contrary pointed to the divergent tradition of the Eastern Churches, even if only, despite strong pressure from Cardinal Bea, in an unbalanced way.

Further, in the 1965 conciliar text, a really biblical basis is given to the state of total abstention – that is, charism not law – which has its origin in the Lord's words in Matthew 19:11f. Wholly in accordance with the eunuch saying of Christ: "He who is able to grasp it, let him

---

29. Wulf in his commentary on PO16 (*loc. cit.* 216ab) calls it, because of its lack of connection with the rest of the text, an "insertion".

30. CT IX, 640.660–669 *passim: 'In 7.* (canone, i.e. the 9th canon of the final text) *tollatur "occidentales"'*.

31. Documentation catholique (Paris), no. 2017, 9 dec. 1990, p.1061 with note 1. See the harsh 'Response' of Jean-Louis Declais, Oran (Algérie), in: Jésus (Paris/Damville), March 1991, p. 32–35.

grasp it", the council says: God can move those who have the "gift of grace"[32] to the celibate state of life, actually to "choose"[33] it. The full text runs: "Total and perpetual continence, highly recommended by the Lord (Matt. 19:12), is not indeed demanded by the very nature of priesthood, as is evident from the practice of the primitive church and from the tradition of the Eastern Churches where alongside those who. . . chose celibacy, there also exist married priests of great merit." With these words in the first section of the conciliar statement both God's freedom of grace and man's freedom of choice are respected. But this respect does not last very long: a little later the "law" which the Latin Church "imposed" is mentioned, thereby posing a contradiction at the outset: In the East they "choose" celibacy, in the West celibacy is "imposed".

b. With the second section we are approaching the celibacy law, because it specifies "the reasons for the *aptness* of priestly celibacy".[34] At this point, we should consider the work of two commentators on the decree, F. Wulf and E. Schillebeeckx.[35] Both of them give the law, newly based on celibacy as "befitting" the priesthood, the awkward interpretation that it should mean an invitation for priests to make the experience of "not being able to be otherwise than remaining unmarried". In other words: the law, they say, seeks to lead priests toward the charismatic ability not to marry. Yet that turns the matter on its head, from both biblical and

---

32. PO 16a.
33. *ibid*.
34. Wulf in his commentary on PO 16, p.219a.
35. Wulf *ibid*.; Schillebeeckx, pp.87ff.

logical viewpoints.[36] A person first makes the experience that he, by grace, cannot but remain unmarried, and only then does he take on the obligation to do so (if he finds it an obligation at all). Either a person has the gift, or he does not have it. According to Matthew 19:11f, the gift of being able to remain unmarried for the sake of the Kingdom is given beforehand.

True, a person can be led to test for himself whether he has the "gift from God", as Paul says in 1 Corinthians 7:7. But is it possible to be invited by a law "through grace not to be able to be otherwise than unmarried", that is, to take possession of the charism itself? Here, that psychological barrier discussed in the Introduction operates as well. The priest to whom the charism of celibacy is given judges from the inside, out of his own experience of not-being-able to be otherwise, an experience which he has received by grace. Therefore, he can hardly put himself in the place of those priests and candidates for the priesthood to whom this charism has not been given, but the other charism of the call to marriage has.[37]

The reasons the council Fathers themselves give for the aptness of celibacy for priesthood is similar. They too were written from the viewpoint of insiders in possession of the charism. That a person can, as they say,

---

36. See above, Ch. 1.
37. See above, Intro. p.1, and p.4 . Cf. M. Thurian, Brother of Taizé, *Ehe und Ehelosigkeit, zwei Dienstordnungen christlichen Lebens* (Gelnhausen-Berlin, undated) pp.50ff: "There must be unrestricted freedom to chose one of these two possibilities (marriage or celibate life). In order to be able to ask for and wish for oneself the gift of celibacy according to Matt. 19:11f, it must, in a way, already have been granted in the form of a promise or a tendency".

"adhere to Christ *more easily* with an undivided heart",[38] when he does not have any familiy, is indeed true – but only for someone who has the charism to "grasp" celibacy. He who has the other "gift from God" according to 1 Corinthinans 7:7, that is the call to marriage, can more easily "adhere to Christ with an undivided heart" within a family. For he would be prevented, by the celibate state to which he is not called, from developing his power to love. He would find it more difficult to love Christ, from within a compulsory state of celibacy, as the neuroses and aberrations among priests show.

Speaking in general terms, celibacy may facilitate the union with Christ "objectively", but judged from the personal gift, marriage makes the union with Christ "subjectively" easier, if that is my personal gift.

The council does not fully exclude this insight: as Schillebeeckx convincingly shows,[39] the council Fathers expressly avoided writing: "They, the celibates, adhere to Christ more easiliy *and* with an undivided heart", because that would mean that only celibate persons could belong to and serve Christ with an undivided heart. The great commandment "to love God with all one's heart" is, however, directed to all, married people also. So it must be possible for them, as well. It is true, Paul does say: "The unmarried man is anxious about the affairs of the Lord, how to please the Lord; but the married man is anxious about worldly affairs, how to please his wife, and so his interests are *divided*" (1 Cor 7:32f). But that is part of his description of the charism's

---

38. PO 16, Abbott, pp. 565–7. Wulf too, *ibid*. 216a, points out that "the anthropological pre-conditions for celibacy" are not taken account of.

39. Schillebeeckx, pp.58,68.

advantages (for the recognition of which he is striving).
He states that, for celibates, it is "easier" to serve Christ
"with an undivided heart". His sentence does not negate
the preceding affirmation in 7:7, that "each has his own
gift from God", marriage or celibacy, which cannot
simply be replaced. Marriage can also be a form of
devotion to the Lord – by means of the devotion to the
partner if it is done "in the Lord": "She is free to be
married, only let it be done in the Lord" (1 Cor. 7:39).

What this sanctification of a marriage through the
Lord looks like is described in the letter to the Ephesians
(5:23ff) and the first letter to the Thessalonians (4:5): it is
by giving up oneself to the marriage partner in the
attitude and power of Christ, without egoistic lust, by
giving instead of taking.

It is essential that we accept the sentence, "there are
varieties of gifts, but the same Spirit, who apportions to
each one as he will" (1 Cor. 12:4.11). If marriage is taken
seriously as a *sacra*-ment, by confessing that it is a
"means of *sancti*-fication", as the Council of Trent does,[40]
it must be attributed the power to sanctify a priest.

So all we need to do is to draw the consequences from
the avoided "*and*" in the conciliar text and to believe that
God can be loved with all one's heart in marriage as well
as in celibacy, and the celibacy problem will be solved.

The conciliar sentence "those who are unmarried can
love Christ *more easily* with an undivided heart" can only
mean that the higher value is put upon the unmarried
state on the basis of an objective category: the charism of
celibacy enjoys precedence over the charism of marriage

---

40. DS 1800f: "*(matrimonium) gratiâ praestat, inter sacramenta
annumerandum.*"

in the Kingdom of God. The grounds for this precedence are laid down in the New Testament (Matt. 19:11f; 1 Cor 7:7; Matt. 19:27: "We have left all"; Luke 14:26): The marital bond must, even where it exists, be subordinate for a shorter or longer time to the service for the Kingdom of God. The precedence is defined by the Council of Trent[41] and has been confirmed by Vatican II in the formula "celibates adhere more easily to Christ". It is not detracted from by the possibility, affirmed by the same council, that Christ can be given undivided love within a family as well. Rather the precedence of celibacy is put in a true light, inasmuch as it is made clear that this way of life is "not" available to "all, but only to those to whom it has been given" (Matt. 19:11). Others, however, have the "other gift" of marriage (1 Cor. 7:7) which is worthy of honour in its own right, among priests as well. And this is stated by the council itself a few lines earlier when it refers to the Eastern Catholic "married priests of outstanding merit"[42].

c. The third section of the conciliar text deals with the law itself, which is justified by the suitability of celibate life for priests. Even if the above (b) mentioned reasons were convincing, what follows from the concept of "befitting" is that it cannot form the basis of a law which is binding for all and which in practice removes the natural rights of priests to marry. For what is appropriate is perhaps very fitting but not exactly absolutely necessary. The Council itself says this a few lines earlier: "Total and perpetual continence... is not demanded by the very nature of priesthood."[43] A law which coerces (*lex*

---

41. DS 1810: *"melius ac beatius"*.
42. PO 16a, cf. above at note 33.
43. *Ibid*.

cogens), in other words, a "must-law" as distinct from a mere "ought-rule",[44] which the celibacy law always has been in the Latin Church since 1139, can, however, by its nature only be justified by a necessity: "The law must be necessary."[45] Otherwise it is not just: "A law is just when it attends to the subjective rights of those affected and allows restrictions of rights solely on higher grounds of the general good. It may not require anything which is against the divine law."[46] The personal freedom of every man to marry *is* of divine law[47] and celibacy *is* not necessary: therefore any lawgiver proposing celibacy as a must-law restricts freedom without good reason; he promulgates an unjust law, a *lex iniqua*. According to the general opinion and to the standards applied by the Church to state laws, such a law is not binding: it is null and void.

We must remember that the Church even nowadays *forbids* marriage for priests and asks only for obedience to this prohibition.[48] To *forbid* marriage is, however, condemned by the Pastoral Letters as being an idea inspired by demons (1 Tim. 4:1–3). The Church does not ask whether the candidate has beforehand freely given up his natural right, which would perhaps be legally admissible if it were possible without a charism.

The council contradicts itself. On the one hand it denies the necessity of celibacy, on the other it lays the legal obligation of it upon all priests. This contradiction is due to the fact that the original reason for the law – to

---

44. Mörsdorf I, 92.
45. B. Häring, Das Gesetz Christi I (Freiburg, 6th ed. 1961), p.315: "The law's object must be just, that is, necessary".
46. Mörsdorf I, 84.
47. See below, chs. 3 and 4.
48. Can. 277 §1 CIC (see above, Intro., n.12).

avoid "impurity" – has disappeared because it is untenable. To avoid something bad is always necessary: therefore, the law seemed to be justified. Now, instead of drawing the consequences of canon law: *Cessante causa cessat lex* – that is, if the reason for a law is proved to be untenable and if consequently there is no necessity left for a general law, the law itself appears unjust and untenable – the council sought to maintain the law intact and support it with a less contestable justification. This was the explicit wish of Pope Paul VI.[49] For him, as has been shown,[50] the old grounds employed from the time of Pope Siricius onwards, at least unconsciously, played a role – concern for the "purity" and "chastity" of priests which all the popes saw endangered by marriage. The council Vatican II could not repeat this reason. Its attempt to justify the law by means of the aptness of unmarried life for priests cannot, however, be regarded as successful, because a must-law can be justified only by a necessity.

d. Still graver is the resulting contradiction between the "gift" and "law" of celibacy, in section 3 which confirms the law. Already the historical survey given by the council as an introduction to the renewed injunction of the law suffers from significant inexactitudes.[51] Even in a summary form, this history cannot be presented as if "celibacy... then... was imposed by law on all who

---

49. Letter of Pope Paul VI to Cardinal E. Tisserant of 10 Oct. 1965, read out on 11 Oct. in the council aula. Cf. LThK Council III, 136; Denzler II, 419,338: A discussion is not to take place. It is the intention of the Pope to retain and affirm the law.

50. See Intro., n. 8.

51. These are admitted also by the commentator on the decree, F. Wulf SJ in: LThK Council III, 220b.

were to be *promoted* to sacred orders".[52] Rather, both in
the fourth century and in the twelfth, it was laid upon
those who *were* already priests, indeed, in their majority
married priests. This is evidenced by the texts of the law
quoted from the time of Pope Siricius and that of the
Lateran Council which forbade already ordained priests,
first to continue in, and then to enter into a marriage.[53] In
the Vatican II account a new interpretation seems to be at
work: the existing law is made into a principle of
selection, which was "imposed" upon those to be
ordained (*promovendis*). This is a further contradiction in
itself: a condition of entry is being set up as a barrier to
the candidates; in historical fact, however, an obligation
was laid upon those who were already ordained. The
true history breaks through the council's wording.

There is no mention here, in the account of the history
of the law, of the gift or charism. Its presence, indeed,
would have to be presupposed in the candidate, if it
were a real principle of selection.

In reality, celibacy was a "professional obligation" of
priests,[54] as evidenced by the law existing at the time of
the council. Canon 132 CIC (1918) in conjunction with
canon 1072 specifies that the higher clergy are "*prevented
from* marrying and bound in such a way by the
obligation to preserve chastity that, when they sin in this,
they are also guilty of sacrilege". No word about
charism, no word about selection; the law, instead,

---

52. PO 16e: *"promovendis lege imposita est"*.
53. DS 119 (D 52c); Conc. Oec. Decr. p.175 (198), see above nn. 4,
15.
54. Mörsdorf I, 261f: "It is not taken over differently from the rest of
the spiritual obligations". Cf. the title of the section in the CIC of 1918:
"De clericorum obligationibus".

pronounces a prohibition of marriage (*a nuptiis arcentur*), which affects those who have been ordained.

We can easily discern the old "cultic" principle of purity as motive for the prohibition: "chastity" is possible only outside marriage. The canon speaks in one breath of "not marrying" and of "chastity". Further, a priest's sin against chastity is designated as a *sacrilege*. Behind this concept we can discover the idea that the priest's body is a "holy thing", a *res oblata*, which is dishonoured by being desecrated through sexual intercourse. Even if we take into consideration that the canon presupposes extra-marital relations as being a sacrilege, why precisely and only should a priest's sexual sin represent a sacrilege, why not every sin? Do not spiritual shortcomings such as loss of faith, lying, breach of the secrecy of confession, simony, do much worse damage to his inextinguishable character of an ordained person? For canon 132 CIC (1918), the body of the priest must be culticly "pure". The hindrance to marriage serves the demand for chastity or "purity". Because of this untenable purpose, the 1918 canon is untenable – a *lex iniqua* – in exactly the same way as are the laws of the fourth and twelfth centuries.

In their attempt to avoid repeating the non-Christian[55] basis of the celibacy law even in their report on its history, the council Fathers of Vatican II were not aware of the consequences that would result from this for a new formulation of the law (can. 132) as required. They did not succeed because Pope Paul did not want any new law.

---

55. Wulf in his commentary on PO 16 admits: the motives are "not always genuinely Christian", or even: "not Christian" (*loc.cit.* p.218a).

e. Having dealt with history, the Fathers addressed themselves to the core of the problem, namely the tension between *law* and *gift* of celibacy. But here, their reconciliation was just as unsuccesful and, indeed, could not succeed, because the two are basically incompatible. Even the German commentator F. Wulf says that here only "is *attempted* an honest answer to the question as to how the fact that priestly celibacy is a grace (according to Matt. 19:11) can be reconciled with a general obligation to celibacy".[56] In Wulf's words, what we have before us "seems not to be an answer" but rather "an uncontrollable reliance upon the Spirit".[57] But the Spirit has already shown us, in scripture and tradition, where we have to look for a solution of the crucial problem of gift and law. According to the New Testament, the charism cannot be obtained by prayer, and this was confirmed indirectly by the Council of Trent when it did not expressly include the ability to obtain it by prayer in its definition.[58]

Now, what does the Second Vatican Council say about the tension between charism and law? "This holy Synod" seeks to harmonize the law, which it "confirms", with "the gift of celibacy", on which it depends, through the fact that it "trusts. . . that the gift of celibacy, which so befits the priesthood of the New Testament, will be generously bestowed by the Father, as long as those who share in Christ's priesthood through the sacrament of

---

56. Wulf, p.217ab.
57. Wulf, *ibid.*, whose opinion is concurred in by W. Seibel SJ, "Die vierte Sitzungsperiode des Konzils", in *Stimmen der Zeit* 177 (1966), p.60: PO 16 "is not one of the best texts of the council".
58. See above, par.3, nn.24–26.

orders, and indeed the whole Church humbly and earnestly pray for it."[59].

This answer is truly surprising coming from a lawgiver: it invites all members of the Church to ask God to help fulfill an untenable obligation. That this is no solution to the problem follows from the further contradiction that earlier, in the account of the law's history, the *candidates* are spoken of as being under the law (*promovendis lege imposita est*); later however, the exhortation to prayer is addressed to already ordained *priests* as those "who share in Christ's priesthood". If the former statement was made with the intention of re-interpreting the law as a principle of selection set up before admission to the priesthood, then the latter faces the problems which the law presents for priests as an obligation of their state. Had the council been coherent in its new interpretation of the law as a principle of selection, then it would have recommended prayer to candidates. When, instead, it encourages those ordained to pray, it takes over the setting of canon 132 CIC (1918) that celibacy is an obligation of the priestly profession.

It is more surprising to learn that those already under the obligation are to pray. When the "synod" exhorts to prayer, it presupposes that the law cannot be fulfilled without the gift. That means, it is aware that it has approved and confirmed a law which cannot be kept without the charism. A just lawgiver would not claim what is beyond the powers of the subordinates themselves. The same rough juxtaposition of law and gift is found in the new canon 277 §1 of the 1983 Code which moulded the conciliar teaching on celibacy into a rule: "Clerics are bound to observe perfect and perpetual

---

59. PO 16e, Abbott, p.566.

restraint for the sake of the Kingdom. Therefore they are obliged to live in celibacy which is a special gift from God". The Code makes no attempt to reconcile gift and obligation.

Accordingly, the obligation inherent in the law as *lex coercens* can be interpreted in two ways only: Either the law seeks to force God to grant to all candidates for priesthood and ordained persons the gift of celibacy; or, it demands from all candidates and those ordained that they wrest the gift from God. The character of this law is compulsion; otherwise it would be no law but only a suggestion.[60] To make prayer a precondition of fulfilling a law, and to force priests to obtain through a compulsory law the uncontrollable charism of the Spirit, "who apportions to each one individually as he will" (1 Cor. 12:11), is in itself so impossible an intention that it can only be supposed the council Fathers were not aware of what they were doing (Luke 23:34).

An unsuspected witness of the impossibility of a law having that intention is the Opus Dei Prelate Alvaro del Portillo. In a 1967 issue of *Seminarium* (the Rome review of the Congregation of Studies) wholly dedicated to the conciliar decree *Presbyterorum Ordinis*,[61] Portillo, at that time an ordinary member of Opus Dei, plainly declared that celibacy cannot be imposed by law. He states: "Every believer is bound to follow his own gift which he received from the Holy Spirit, see 1 Cor. 7:7": "one of this kind, one of another".[62] The immediate consequence should be that a law of celibacy is impossible: No one can

---

60. Cf. Mörsdorf I,6f,83f: see above n.44.
61. A. Portillo, "Caelibatus sacerdotalis in Decreto conciliario *Presbyterorum Ordinis*", in *Seminarium* 19 (1967) 711–28, quotations pp.717,725.
62. See above ch.1, par.2.

claim that everyone has the same charism of celibacy. In fact, Portillo continues to ask: "Is it possible to impose celibacy by a human law? Undoubtedly the answer must be negative. Precisely for this reason the decree Presb. Ord. n. 16 starts by reminding us of the fact that perfect and constant continence for the sake of the Kingdom is a divine gift that God grants to whom He will. It is a *donum gratis datum*. Therefore, the ecclesiastical authority cannot give, even less impose, what it does not have." This is clear enough. But then he explicitly shows that the intention of the lawgiver was to interpret the law afresh as a principle of selection: "The authority can, however, state that the previous reception of this gift is a necessary *condition of access* to holy orders for the faithful. And that is what is meant by the law of celibacy."

In fact, the law was not introduced as a means of selection but rather as an obligation. Therefore this interpretation is unacceptable. It is also impossible: if the Church chooses from possible candidates only the celibates, there is no escape from the conclusion that the Latin Church itself rejects divine vocations to the priesthood, since it is obvious that God calls to the priesthood married people as well. This is declared in the same conciliar decree (PO 16): "Continence. . . is not indeed demanded by the very nature of the priesthood, as is evident from the practice of the primitive Church and from the tradition of the Eastern Churches. . . (where) there also exist married priests of great merit."[63]. If God at any rate chooses priests in the conjugal state, how can the Latin Church reject them by selection? For this reason, as well, Portillo's interpretation is im-

---

63. PO 16a, Abbott, p.565.

possible. In any case, the present head of Opus Dei has stated that celibacy cannot be imposed by law.

It is evident that the position of the Vatican Council was as follows: the law was in existence; in accordance with the Pope's wish it was not to be changed, nor even discussed; the old basis has become obsolete; hence an attempt is made to provide a new one, which, however, cannot shore up the existing law. The charism necessary for the keeping of the law *is* not amenable to a law, according to Matthew 19:11 not even to prayer. Hence the principle of legal theory applies: "In order for a law to have obligatory force, it must be a reasonable ordinance. With regard to whether it can be followed, a law is reasonable when what it commands is not merely physically but morally *possible*, and that with regard to the *capacity* of the person affected. *Ad impossibile nemo tenetur.*"[64]

Since the charism, the "capacity" for a celibate life, is not at the disposal of the individual affected, the law exceeds the capacity of many persons subject to it. For all those who do not have the charism, no legal obligation comes into force. Since, however, the law is intended to be binding on all priests, but not all priests have the charism, as the papal authorities through their many dispensations since 1964 (60,000 up to 1991)[65] themselves indisputably show, the law *cannot* reach its objective of obliging all priests to be celibate. It must, therefore, be repealed as an "unreasonable, irrational law".

---

64. Mörsdorf I, 84; Häring I, 309: "A law which is morally or physically impossible has no binding force".
65. Cf. *Il Mattino* 30 Aug. 1991, p.8, declaration of Mgr Simcic from the Congregation of Clergy.

We are bound to take Christ's words seriously: "Not all men are capable of making this real but only those to whom it has been given". "Not all men" includes, according to the conciliar text itself: not all priests, since the council alludes to "married priests of great merit", whom it encourages to "persevere in their vocation".[66] It is hard to see how the council, a few lines later, can "confirm" the law for *all* who are to be "promoted" to holy orders, and whence it derives the "trust", that "the gift of celibacy... will be generously bestowed by the Father (on) those who share in Christ's priesthood through the sacrament of orders."[67] It is remarkable that it obliges "all" by its law, while it cannot assure that the Father will give the call to the celibate life "to *all*" but only "*generously*"! Without being sure about the pre-conditions, one cannot establish a general command. And how does the council know that the Father acts differently in the East from in the West when sharing out his spiritual gifts? Must we not adapt Paul's question: "Is God the God of Jews only? Is he not the God of Gentiles also? Yes, of Gentiles also, since God is one" (Rom. 3:29f). If God calls married men to the priesthood in the East, he certainly does so in the West, as well. God cannot be made into a *deus ex machina* for the purpose of an unresolved legal problem, and God cannot be expected to make the unfulfillable demand of the law fulfillable for the purposes of the Latin West only. God is not partial but just.

And even as a human lawgiver, the Latin Church must be just and respect the earthly principle of the *aequitas canonica*: "Justice demands that equal things are treated

---

66. PO 16e.
67. *Ibid.*.

equally."[68] Admission to the priesthood is such a matter which, for the sake of justice, would have to be treated equally. The violation of this principle represents a further reason why the law of celibacy is unjust, a *lex iniqua*, in short null and void.[69]

The internal contradictions in PO 16 continue. Toward the end, priests are urged to "persevere faithfully" in the celibate state, "and recognize this surpassing gift of grace which the Father *has* given them". Just before this, they had been exhorted to pray for it; now it is presupposed that they already have the gift. Again the question arises whether so contradictory a text is suited "to give an answer to the question, heard again and again and which has become so central to the celibacy discussion, that is, how a special gift which God grants to a *few* (as the council says itself in Lumen gentium 42), can be made the object of a *general* law".[70]

Just these last words of the council on the relationship between gift of celibacy and calling to the priesthood demonstrate that the consequences of the "eunuch-saying" of Christ were not seen by the council Fathers: "this surpassing gift of grace which the Father has given them and which the Lord so openly praised, cf. Matt.

---

68. Mörsdorf I, 113. Cf. H. Weinkauff (former judge of the German constitutional court), "Widerstandsrecht", in *Staatslexikon* VIII (Freiburg, 1963), p.681: "The 'equality axiom' applies as a natural barrier against the power of the state (and Church, we add), the clear abuse of which gives rise to the right of opposition", because it is "the formal basis of the law of *every legal system*"; it "states: matters which because of their nature and for the sake of justice, are to be treated equally in law, may not be treated unequally in law".
69. See above, nn. 45–6.
70. F. Wulf in his commentary on PO 16: LThK Council III, 220a.

19:11".[71] It is obviously not noticed here that the Lord's saying does not invite someone to prayer but simply states the fact of a few by grace being able to live an unmarried life, and further, that Christ's saying in the context of Matthew's Gospel does not betray any specific connection with the ministry in the Church or with priesthood. Rather, on the one hand, solitude is a special vocation: monks and nuns of later times up to the present day refrain from marriage due to their divine calling – and these brothers and sisters of religious orders originally did not want to become priests. On the other hand, the Apostles who are to be reckoned as certainly the first to hear the eunuch-saying were married, for the most part at least: not only Peter, whose mother-in-law was the first woman to have been cured by Jesus (Mark 1:30 par.), but also Philip, and Jude, the "Lord's brother" (1 Cor. 9:5). They all were unable to apply the sentence on "eunuchs for the sake of the Kingdom" to themselves who were married, and, nevertheless, chosen by the Lord to be the future office-holders of the Church. This draws our attention to the exegetical questions connected with St Paul's words in 1 Corinthians 9:5 on the right of the apostles to be accompanied by a wife (chapter 3) and their effect on the law of celibacy (chapter 4).

---

71. PO 16f; compare 16a.

Chapter 3

The Apostles' Right to take Their Wives with Them

The fact that the charism of celibacy is not attainable by asking reflects, also, each apostle's right to take his wife with him: a priest who has not received the gift of celibacy, of course has the natural and spiritual right to live in the sacrament of marriage, just as Paul says in 1 Corinthians 7:7: "Each one has his own gift from God, one of this kind, one of another."[1]

Before turning to the exegesis of St Paul's words stating this right, a critical review of the text of 1 Corinthians 9:5 is necessary, as the centuries have left their mark on this sentence, for understandable reasons. Surprisingly enough, Paul in this verse claims as an apostolic right: "Do we perhaps not have the full power to take along with us a sister (in faith) as wife, just as the other apostles do, and the brethren of the Lord, and Peter?"

1. According to the findings of G. Zuntz,[2] the original text must have spoken, in the decisive passage, of the

---

1. See above, ch.1, par.2.
2. G. Zuntz, *The Text of the Epistles* (London, 1953), p.138, quoted in J.B. Bauer, *"Uxores circumducere (1 Kor 9:5)"*, in *Biblische Zeitschrift, Neue Folge*, 3 (1959) 94f.

right to take *women* along (*gynaîkas periágein*), in the plural and without the addition of *sisters* (*adelphàs*). The later *textus receptus* reads: *adelphèn gynaîka periágein*, "have a sister as wife", which, however, does not change the meaning essentially, because "sister" is understood a fellow-Christian. The meaning of "wife" given to the word "woman" remains unaffected by this. If, together with "sister" stress is also laid on "woman", and if, quite possibly, that is the more original word, then doubtless what is meant by the female companion of the apostles, is their wife. We shall return to this in the exegesis.

Zuntz adduces the following reason for the preference for the shorter text *gynaîkas*: Witnesses to the short text "*Uxores circumducere*" as far apart and as early as Tertullian of Carthage (died about 220), Clement of Alexandria (died about 215), Hilary of Poitiers (died 367) and the Persian sage Aphrahat (died in 345) – to whose number we can add Ambrosiaster (between 366 and 384) and the early Jerome in *Adversus Helvidium* (383) and *Epistula 22* (384) – cannot have obtained their text from mutual information: it must go back to a time in which copies of such widely distributed manuscripts were still being made from a common source, namely, from a manuscript of great antiquity, reaching back to the second century. The oldest manuscripts handed down to us, above all Papyrus 46, stem only from the third century, all others date from the fourth and fifth centuries: they contain the longer text.

So, the reading witnessed to by these early church Fathers is to be given preference, primarily for the external reason that it is the older reading. It is also found in two manuscripts of the ninth century, called Boernerianus (G) and Augiensis (F) which, because of the parallel Old Latin version copied in conjunction, have often kept old readings in the Greek text too.[3]

An internal piece of evidence also argues for the shorter text: the singular of the later *textus receptus* is probably due to the attempt to preclude the idea of polygamy among the apostles, as if each were taking several women (plural) with him. And the word "sister" might have been added in explanation and for reasons of decency: of course, the wife had to be a Christian believer. The opposite development, the cancelling of "sister" from the original text and the changing of the singular into the plural, would, however, not be understandable: the shorter and more difficult reading is generally regarded as the older one. So, the text attested by Clement and Tertullian at the end of the second century can be relied on with great certainty. In any case, it is to be noted, that the earliest church Fathers translate the term *gynaîkas*, which occurs in both readings, without exception as *uxores*, wives.

The latest reading of the Vulgata-Clementina, dating from 1592, when it was issued as the official Latin bible translation following the council of Trent, which declared Jerome's translation as "authentic",[4] needs a discussion to itself. This late edition reverses the word-order of the longer text: *sororem mulierem circumducendi*, to take along with us a sister as woman, and reads it the

---

3. Cf. the copius citations of manuscripts and quotations from the Fathers in the apparatus of J. Wordsworth-H.J. White, *Novum Testamentum Domini Nostri Jesu Christi Latine secundum Editionem Sancti Hieronymi*, tom. II (Oxford, 1913ff), pp.219f. The chronological details of codices and writings of the Fathers are taken in what follows from *Vetus Latina, Die Reste der altlateinischen Bibel. Nach P. Sabatier neu gesammelt und herausgegeben von der Erzabtei Beuron*, vol.I (Freiburg, 1949), and from J. P. Migne, *Patrologia, Series Latina* (PL), vol.23.
4. DS 1506.

other way round: *mulierem sororem circumducendi*, to take along a woman as sister, which indeed brings about a considerable change in sense.

Just as the double accusative in Matthew 1:20: *mè phobetès paralabeîn Marían tèn gynaîká sou*, or in Latin: *noli timere accipere Mariam conjugem tuam*, has to be translated: "Do not fear to take Mary *as* your wife", so also in 1 Corinthians 9:5 *sororem mulierem circumducere* is to be rendered by "To take for a companion a sister *as* woman" or wife. The reversal makes this interpretation, in any case, impossible. Neither does it produce any clear meaning: "To take along a woman as sister" – what is this supposed to mean? "A woman *as* Christian" makes no sense. "A woman only as if she were sister (by birth)" is obviously what it is meant to say, but that cannot possibly be Paul's intention; it would push the "spiritual marriages" of the third century back into the apostolic age. "A woman as 'sister'" (in an order) would finally be a worse anachronism still: religious orders for women date from the sixth century only.

Jerome (347–420), who is regarded up till now as the author of the Latin Vulgate translation,[5] does not know of this change. His text, however, according to the decree of Trent, was, in 1592, "to be printed as correctly as possible without mistakes".[6] It is true that in his later writings Jerome prefers the translation *sorores mulieres* (sisters as women) instead of the shorter earlier reading *uxores* (wives),[7] for which change – in the absence of

---

5. Cf. however H.J. Frede, *Der Brief an die Epheser*, in *Vetus Latina* 24/1 (Freiburg, 1962), Foreword.

6. DS 1508.

7. Hieronymus, *Adversus Helvidium* 11: PL 23 (1845) 194B, (1883) 204A, from the year 383: "*uxores circumducendi*"; ten years later, in 393, he writes in *Adversus Jovinianum* 1,26: "*sorores mulieres circumducendi*".

Latin manuscripts which read in this way – he relies on Greek codices which contain the longer text. But in all his texts he adheres to the word-order: sisters as women, *sorores mulieres*, found in both the Greek and Latin manuscripts available to him, and not the other way round. So the editors of the Vulgate were not able to appeal to Jerome, whose works they certainly exploited, when editing the text to *mulierem sororem*. Even the manuscripts of the Vulgate itself available to them, which included the famous Codex Amiatinus,[8] almost unanimously follow the word-order of Jerome's works and of the Greek manuscripts: *sororem mulierem*. The more recent critical edition of the Vulgate by Wordsworth-White[9] in 1913 can enumerate only two out of thirty manuscripts which have the transposition altering the sense: *mulierem sororem*. But even given the state of knowledge in their times, the 1592 editors were not really able to lay much emphasis on these two, relatively worthless, manuscripts, since they themselves preferred the reading of the Codex Amiatinus in all instances. By departing from this guide here, they clearly did so not on grounds of textual criticism, but because of a specific intention. This can be guessed with a high degree of probability: the editors sought to veil, as far as possible, by means of the transposition, the obvious meaning of the original wording: "Do we not have the right to be accompanied by a wife, as the other apostles?" on account of the canon law then in force, which forbade precisely that to the apostles' successors in the Latin West.

---

8. Cf. K.Th. Schäfer, *Grundriß der Einleitung in das Neue Testament* (Bonn, 2nd ed. 1952), pp.40f.
9. See above, n.3.

By this device, the Vulgate Commission of 1592 unwillingly became a witness to the extraordinary importance of Paul's words. Had the Commission not realized that this one sentence, should it have become better known, had the power to bring down the whole structure of the Latin discipline of celibacy, then it would probably not have taken it upon itself to change the wording and meaning of a scriptural text, contrary to the Greek original, against the text of Jerome, and in disagreement with the virtually unanimous witness of the Vulgate manuscripts.

That this Pauline statement is still so little known is due, not least, to the transposition in the "official" Vulgate which has for four hundred years since been regarded as the authentic text, although it does not correspond to Jerome's Vulgate or to the Bible.

In this case it is somewhat difficult to believe in the good faith of the Commission. Certainly, its intention was to be obedient to the Church and its law. Obedience to the written word of God, however, undoubtedly deserves to be placed higher – as witness the New Testament teaching on Peter resisting the High Priests (cf. Acts 4:19; 5:29). The "right to be accompanied by a wife", which Paul has "as well as the other apostles and the brothers of the Lord and Peter/Cephas", obviously deprives the Church laws of all justification: neither the "prohibition to have children" (fourth century), nor the declaration making priestly marriages null and void (twelfth century), nor the marital obstacle of ordination (Trent, sixteenth century) are legitimate when seen against the background of the apostolic right.

2. After this glance at the history of the text, we can now turn to the text's meaning.

a. The oldest witness to the text, Tertullian, also gives the oldest and, therefore, probably the most unbiased interpretation. He writes, in *De exhortatione castitatis* 8 (around 204): "The apostles too were allowed to marry and take their wives with them".[10] There is no doubt that this is a quotation from 1 Corinthians 9:5; this is clear from the actual words used: *licebat* rendering the *exousía* or *potestas*; *apostolis*, which occurs in the verse; *uxores* rendering *gynaikas*; *circumducere* rendering *periagein*; it follows from the next sentence in Tertullian: "They were also allowed to live from the Gospel", *licebat et de evangelio ali*, which is a quotation summarizing the verses which precede and follow in Paul's letter, 9:4–14. It is strange and significant at the same time that Tertullian adds to the words of Paul in 9:5: "They had the right to *marry*", while strictly speaking Paul stresses only their right to be accompanied by the wife they already married. Thus Tertullian testifies to the *natural right* of the apostles, even though in the context he opts, himself, for not marrying.

Thirteen years later Tertullian changed his view about the passage. This obviously took place in the context of his turning to rigoristic Montanism which took place around 205, after which he adhered to this sect to his death. Now, in *De monogamia* 8,6,[11] which is to be dated around the year 217,[12] he is unable to attribute wives to the apostles in 1 Corinthians 9:5, but he sees in the *gynaîkes* "women who served them". The intention, born

---

10. *Corpus Christianorum* (CC) II, 1026f; *Corpus Scriptorum Ecclesiasticorum Latinorum* (CSEL) 70, 141: "*Licebat et apostolis nubere et uxores circumducere*". Cf. *De pudicitia* 14,11: CC II, 1307f.
11. CC II, 1239f.
12. See *Vetus Latina* I, 101f: *De exh. cast.* was written "around 204/7", *De monog.* "around 217".

of heretical rigorism, is clear: the Montanist hostility to marriage made its mark on Tertullian and influenced his exegesis. It is neither original nor reliable.

Clement of Alexandria (before 215), on the contrary, in *Paedagogos* II,1,9,[13] places the "being accompanied by wives" on the same level with the "eating and drinking" of 1 Corinthians 9:4, both being a "neutral usage", in other words: natural rights. In his work *Stromateis* III,6,52,[14] he even thinks that it is possible to infer from Philippians 4:3, that Paul had a wife, who, admittedly, did not travel with him, because she could not serve him on the mission. He adduces as evidence for this 1 Corinthians 9:5. This interpretation, however, goes against the assertion elsewhere by the apostle that he is unmarried (1 Cor. 7:7). Still, it does show how *gynaîka* was understood at the end of the second century: as "wife".

There is another witness to this meaning in the third century: Eusebius of Caesarea (265–335). Although he did not actually examine this verse, he tells us something about the fact that the apostles had wives. According to him, the apostle Philip had three daughters.[15] And he tells us the story of the two grandchildren of Judas Thaddaeus, the Lord's brother, who were sent to Rome for martyrdom as Christians, but sent back when the

---

13. Migne, *Patrologia, Series Graeca* (PG) 8, 392B.
14. PG 8, 1156f.
15. Eusebius of Caesarea, *Historia ecclesiastica* III,31,2–3. The daughters of the apostle Philip mentioned here cannot be identical, as is often claimed, with the four daughters of the *deacon* Philip in Acts 21,9, because there were three of them; besides, those of the deacon were virgins, according to Acts, whereas one of the apostle's daughters was married, according to Eusebius.

judge saw their calloused hands.[16] Anyone who has sons
and grandsons has obviously been married.

Bishop Hilary of Poitiers (310–67), in his commentary
on the Psalms, speaks in terms very similar to the earliest
interpreters about "the apostles' right to marry": "When
the apostle praises abstinence, at the same time he does
not put anything in the way of the right to marry; he only
draws on the value of celibacy. . .: Do we not have the
right to take women with us just as the other apostles
and the brethren of the Lord and Cephas?"[17] So, he
understands 1 Corinthians 9:5 in such a way that the
natural "right to marry" is expressedly stated as that of
the apostles as well. We have to give all the more weight
to this exegesis by a canonized Father of the Church,
raised to the rank of *Doctor Ecclesiae* in 1851, because it
was made before the letter of Pope Siricius to Himerius
of Spain in 385, which made abstinence an obligation
upon the clergy: Hilary wrote at a time when there was
no law that influenced the interpretation.

Against this, Jerome (347–420) is clearly influenced by
the legislation. *Before* the pope's letter tȯ Himerius of
Tarragona (385),[18] in *Adversus Helvidium* 11 (383),[19] he
copies in his reply to Helvidius the text of his adversary
word for word, *"uxores circumducere"*, without criticizing
it. However, *after* the papal letter, in *Adversus Jovinianum*

---

16. Eusebius, *Hist. eccl.* III,20,1–5.
17. Hilarius, *Tractatus in psalmos*, Ps. 118 Nun 14: CSEL 22, 483, 8–17:
*"Apostolus, cum continentiam laudat, non inhibet iam potestatem nubendi,
sed meritum caelibatus praedicat. . .: Numquid non habemus potestatem
mulieres circumducendi sicut et ceteri apostoli et fratres domini et
Cephas?"*
18. DS 185, see above ch.2, n.3.
19. PL 23 (1845) 194B, (1883) 204A. Cf. *Epistula* 2,20: CSEL 54,171; PL
23, 407, dating from the year 384.

1,26 (in 393),[20] he prefers to translate *gynaîkas* by "*mulieres*", women, rather than by "*uxores*", wives, "because *gyné* means both among the Greeks"; besides, he thinks Jovinian has to add the word found in the Greek manuscripts, *sorores*: from this "it follows that he is speaking about other holy women who helped them with their valuables, as indeed we read, that the Lord too was served by women", and he refers to Luke 8:1–3.

To follow C. Spicq and J. B. Bauer: there is a purpose behind this interpretation.[21] It was intended to counter, by scriptural authority, the celibacy crisis caused by Jovinian's espousal of the equal value of marriage and virginity in Rome around 390. Yet even apart from this purpose infecting the meaning given by Jerome, it is also factually untenable, for the "women, who followed the Lord and provided for" him and his disciples (Luke 8:2–3), are not the object of a *right* of the apostles, about which Paul speaks in 1 Corinthians 9:5. Nobody has a right to a housekeeper or maid-servant, least of all the servants of Christ, since "the Son of man also came not to be served but to serve" (Mark 10:45 par), and "a disciple is not above his teacher" (Matt. 10:24 par). There is, indeed, a kind of right to "get one's living by the Gospel" (1 Cor. 9:14) which was established and also made use of by the Lord, for which Luke 10:7 and 8:3 provide the proof. Thus, the women in Luke 8:3 are rather a parallel to 1 Corinthians 9:4–14 than to 9:5. Among Christians, the right of a man to a woman is based solely on marriage. The women spoken of in 1 Corinthians 9:5, to whom the apostles had a "right",

---

20. PL 23, 245B (257A).
21. C. Spicq, *Epîtres aux Corinthiens: La Sainte Bible* (Pirot-Clamer) XIb (Paris, 1951), p.230a. – Bauer: See above, note 2.

must have been the apostles' wives. And such they were, according to our historical knowledge about Peter, Philip and Jude.

It is clear, then, that either rigorism (in Tertullian), or the Latin canon law (in Jerome), influenced the natural and original understanding of the text presented by both Fathers in their early writings, as well as by Clement and Hilary. The reason for the change was the wish to eliminate the "apostles' wives" who were regarded as an offence in the fourth century only because they appeared to contradict the well-known encratitic tendencies of that time. Preference, of course, is to be given to the natural, earlier interpretation.

All later church writers were influenced by the direction Jerome gave to the interpretation, when he pointed to the women rendering service to Jesus and his apostles, in Luke 8:3. We need not, therefore, consider them in detail.[22]

One remark, however, must be made on the thesis of J. Galot that at the time of their being called by Jesus, none of the apostles was married.[23] A response might be[24] that Galot has neglected much of the evidence quoted above. Above all, he fails to take into account Tertullian's text: "Even the apostles were allowed to marry and take their wives with them" (*Exh. cast.* 8). Another instance of the continuing conviction of the Church that 1 Corinthians 9:5 speaks of the wives of the apostles, is Humbert of

---

22. On the further history of exegesis, cf. for instance R. Cornely, *Commentarius in S. Pauli Apostoli Epistulas II, Prior Epistula ad Corinthios*: Cursus Scripturae Sacrae (Paris, 1890), pp.237ff.

23. J. Galot SJ, "Lo stato di vita degli apostoli", in *La Civiltà cattolica* no. 3346 (18 Nov. 1989).

24. H.-J. Vogels, "Le mogli degli apostoli", in *Vita pastorale* (Nov. 1990) p.56.

Silva Candida's letter to Abbot Niketas from the year 1054, reproduced in the *Decretum Gratiani*,[25] where he admits the right of priests to have "wives, *uxores*, as we read that the apostles had, since the apostle Paul says: Do we not have the right, etc." (1 Cor. 9:5 follows). Though he denies that they had marital intercourse, at least he admits the juridical importance of the text for the later canon law (we are still before Lateran II in 1139!). There is no escape from trusting Paul's evidence that he knew the apostles' "wives".

b. The present discussion has been described fully by J.B. Bauer in his article *"Uxores circumducere"*.[26] The meaning "wives" is gaining ground. O. Kuss,[27] J. Kürzinger,[28] C. Spicq and E.-B. Allo[29] also reckon with the possibility that wives are meant; in their view, however, it is more likely that the broader term "woman" is intended. H. D. Wendland has given the debate a new tone.[30] It is not the right to marry that Paul is speaking of but the right to support from the

---

25. *Decretum* D.32 c.11: Friedberg I,114.
26. *Biblische Zeitschrift*, NF 3 (1959) 94–102.
27. O. Kuss, *Die Briefe an die Roemer, Korinther und Galater*: RNT 6 (Regensburg, 1940) p.154.
28. J. Kürzinger, *Die Briefe an die Korinther und Galater*: Echterbibel 4 (Würzburg, 1954) pp.23f. In the new edition: Die neue Echterbibel, 1. *Korintherbrief* (Würzburg, 1984) p.64, Hans-J. Klauck adopts the term "wives of the apostles" without discussion. It is a pity, though, that he neglects the term "right".
29. See above, n.21; E.-B. Allo, *Première Epître aux Corinthiens: Etudes Bibliques* (Paris, 2nd ed. 1956) pp.212ff.
30. H.D. Wendland, *Die Briefe an die Korinther: Das Neue Testament Deutsch* (NTD) 7 (Göttingen, 12th ed. 1968) p.71. His view was taken over by W.G. Kümmel, *An die Korinther I.II: Handbuch zum Neuen Testament* 9 (Tübingen, 5th ed. 1969) pp.39f, and by Fr. Lang, *Die Briefe an die Korinther*: NTD 7 (Göttingen-Zürich, 1986) p.119. Both of them translate "wives".

communities. This Paul deals with in the context of 1 Corinthians 9:4, 6–14, and the right to have a companion is only mentioned in passing. The sense of this passing reference is that the apostles were able to demand from the churches that they maintain their wives also.

Against this, it can rightly be asserted that Paul then, at least indirectly, still speaks of a right to a wife. For, if he and Barnabas have the right to be accompanied by a wife, then they must also have the preceding right to choose a wife for themselves, that is to marry. Otherwise they would not really have the right to take a wife with them.

Paul has immediately before, in chapter 7 of 1 Corinthians, spoken of the right to marry. So more lengthy consideration was not necessary in 9:5. Further, it is to be noted that Paul, after having listed his "rights" in 9:4–14, speaks in verse 15 of "several" rights which he declined to make use of: "Yet I have made no use of any of these (freedoms)", *ou kéchremai oudenì toútōn*. Hence he was not speaking, before, of only one right – that of being provided for – but of various rights.[31]

In view of the probable shorter original text *gynaîkas* and the undoubted original meaning *uxores*, wives, there is no need of further argument to establish the result of these exegetical endeavours: in his letter to the Corinthians Paul speaks of the actual custom of several, specifically named apostles, Peter and the brothers of the

---

31. J.B. Bauer (see n.2) points to the occurrence in the classical and in the biblical realm of the triad "Eating, drinking, marrying" which are the fundamental requirements of life. Jesus uses it in Matt. 24,37f par: "In those days before the flood they were eating and drinking, marrying and giving in marriage". Yet this is only in a very general sense what Paul means when he speaks of the specific apostolic rights.

Lord and other apostles,[32] to take their wives with them on missionary journeys, and their right to require food and drink for them from the churches, in the same way as they could for themselves. Even preferring the longer text "a sister as wife", this interpretation does not alter, because the object of an apostolic "right" could only be a *wife* – naturally a Christian one, hence a "sister" – not however a serving maid.

c. Now, the definition of this right is as follows: *exousía* means quite generally "permission, right", derived from *éxestin*, "it is allowed". In the New Testament, *exousía* always means a full power derived from God.[33] In 1 Corinthians 9, however, Paul lists special rights held by the *apostles*. They are held by him "as the other apostles" by the fact of being an apostle and office-holder; these are not rights shared by all Christians! All Christians cannot claim support from the churches.

Accordingly, Paul begins chapter 9, which deals with his rights and his voluntary restraint from their use (as an example for voluntary restraint by the Corinthians), with the threefold question: "Am I not *free*? Am I not an *apostle*? Have I not seen Jesus our *Lord*?" (1 Cor. 9:1). In the first question he sums up his rights; with the second he stresses his authority as an apostle; with the third he founds his authority on the Lord who called him.

In the context of chapters 8–10, dealing with the divine right of the Corinthians to eat flesh coming from

---

32. We can omit the question of the identity of the "Apostles" and the "Twelve", often debated in the last years, since Paul in any case stresses the rights of the "office-holders" in the young church, to whom he as well as the apostles named certainly belong.

33. Cf. *Theologisches Wörterbuch zum Neuen Testament*, ed. G. Kittel and H. Friedrich (Stuttgart, 1933ff) 2, 563.

sacrifices to the idols, Pauls seeks to say in chapter 9: I
want to give you an example as to what you should do
with your right to eat flesh offered to the idols and then
sold on the market: you have the right to eat it because
there are no idols, they do not exist. But if someone is
weak and does not believe in the nullity of idols, and
therefore takes offence at your meal, then you should
rather refrain from eating, for love of your brother who
thinks you worship idols. In the same way I am free in
many ways as an apostle, but I do not make use of my
rights, in order to win many for the Gospel (9:15, 19).
What follows is, thus, concerned with freedoms or
subjective rights held by him as an apostle and founded
on the authority of the Lord, who called him to be an
apostle.

This tracing back of the anchor of his rights to their
ultimate basis in the will of the *Lord* is of vital
significance for their evaluation: just as the Corinthians
have the right before *God* (in "conscience", 10:25) to eat
flesh offered to the idols, so the specific apostolic rights
are of *divine origin*. Paul stresses this once more expressly
at the end of the passage (9:14): "In the same way, the
Lord commanded that those who proclaim the gospel
should live from the gospel." This refers to the right,
named first (9:4), of being provided for by the churches:
"Do we not have the right to our food and drink?" with
which Paul alludes to the saying of the Lord in Luke 10:7
(par. Matt. 10:10): "Eat and drink what they provide, for
the labourer deserves his wages". The second right (9:5)
is introduced in just as challenging and urgent a way as
the first: "Do we perhaps not have the right to take wives
with us?", *mè ouk échomen exousían gynaîkas periágein?*
This refers to the accompanying wives who share in the
apostles' right to food and drink. The connection with

this special apostolic right of support is the reason why
Paul mentions the right to be accompanied by wives: the
wives of preachers are intensively involved in the service
of preaching; therefore, the same reward is due to them
as well.[34] Now, if the first apostolic right "to food and
drink" goes back to the Lord, the second in the mind of
Paul, of course, goes back to the same Lord. The apostles
"have" the rights, they do not usurp it. And they "have"
it from the Lord, that to eat and drink explicitly (see Luke
10:7), that to a companion implicitly and by nature,
created by the same Lord (see Gen. 1:28; 2:24; 1 Cor.
7:9.39). The third right derives from the first: the
apostles, occupied with the mission, need not work with
their own hands: "Or is it only Barnabas and I who have
not the right to refrain from working?" (9:6), but to live
from their gifts, from "church taxes" or "from the
gospel", as the Lord says.

Thus, the three rights are founded in the will of Christ,
the Lord. We are dealing with the God-given law
guaranteed by the Lord – in technical language, with the
ius divinum.

We can sense the care of the Lord, who wanted to
protect his apostles – and their successors and helpers,
like Barnabas – from being over-exerted by having two
jobs, and by celibacy which not all can bear (see Matt.
19:11). As Paul and others show, the divine "right" does
not, indeed, rule out voluntary refraining, "not to make
use of the right" (1 Cor 9:15). Yet they retain the
"freedom" even when they have refrained, otherwise
Paul could not stress his rights after having refrained.
The other apostles, as well, had refrained from their

---

34. In Protestant and Eastern Churches they even take over the
professional name of their husbands: *episcopa, presbytera,* etc.

marital rights for some time: "We have left everything (and everyone) and followed you: what shall be our reward?", Peter asks Jesus (Matt. 19:29), because no earthly tie can claim precedence over Christ and the gospel. However, after the Lord's ascension, "the other apostles and the brothers of the Lord and Cephas/Peter" started again to live with their "wives", and took them around on their missionary journeys, as Paul tells us in 1 Corinthians 9:5.

This means the apostles as well as Paul are, at any time, free to make use of the right to take a wife with them, because of the help she is able to give in the spreading of the gospel.

The actual possibility of making, at any time, use of his rights, is one of the reasons why Paul speaks of his rights at all: he insists on "having" the same rights as the other apostles, on account of equality of status with them. He is not inferior to them in the matter of authority and rights. So he stresses: "If to others I am not an apostle, at least I am to you; this is my defence to those who would examine me: Do we not have the right to our food and drink? Do we not have the right to be accompanied by a wife? Or are Barnabas and I the only ones not to have the right to refrain from working? While the other apostles have it?" (1 Cor. 9:2–6). It is clear that he is using his rights so as to show that his apostolic authority is identical to that of the other apostles. It is crucial that these are *real* rights and can be exercised at any time. He still "has" the right to chose a wife as his companion, is not bound once and for all because he has renounced the use of his right: he remains "free" (9:1). When he refrains, it is his boast (9:15).

We have to keep this in mind with regard to the problem of marriage after ordination:[35] According to

Paul, any successor of the apostles, any priest, may marry even after ordination.

d. To sum up: we can state whenever the word *gyné* in the Greek New Testament is found to have a connection to a man, an *anér*, it always has the meaning "wife", as indeed in many languages "my woman" means "my wife". So, for instance, we read in 1 Corinthians 7:2: "Each man should have his own woman". Then, in 1 Corinthians 9:5, the same word *gyné* which appears in close connection with men who take her as companion, can refer only to the apostles' wife.[36] As the Gospel of Mark shows (1:30) and Eusebius proves in his Church History (III,20,1–5 and 31,2–3), some of the apostles mentioned in 1 Corinthians 9:5 were at some time married. This suggests that Paul is here alluding to the apostles' wives. In fact, the oldest witnesses, Tertullian, Clement, the Old Latin translation, Hilary and the early Jerome, translated and interpreted the word *gyné* as *uxores*, wives. The later translation *mulieres*, women, and the interpretation which made them "women who

---

35. Cf. R.Clement, *Dialoghi con Atenagora* (Turin, 1972), p.191ff: the famous Patriarch Athenagoras of Constantinople had in mind "la riforma che consentirebbe al prete di sposarsi dopo l'ordinazione. . .Ma perchè non ammettere vescovi sposati? San Paolo ci dice che Pietro e gli altri apostoli avevano ognuno la propria compagna", which is a clear allusion to 1 Cor. 9:5. We learn that the Patriarch too wished to draw legal consequences for the orthodox Church from that passage: "Un uomo che si vota al servizio della Chiesa deve poter scegliere liberamente di sposarsi o non sposarsi" ("A man who is prepared to serve the Church must be free to chose either marriage or not marrying").

36. Cf. H.-J. Vogels, "O sentido de 1 Corintios 9:5" in *Atualidades Biblicas* (Sâo Paolo, 1971) p.558–71. See the book review of the German version by Suitbertus a S. Joanne a Cruce in: *Ephemerides Carmeliticae* XII (Rome, 1961) pp.476–8.

helped", was influenced either by heresy (in Tertullian) or by the legislation on continence (in Jerome). The probably secondary addition *adelphén* or *sororem*, sister, occurred on grounds of decency or, in the West, to weaken the meaning "wife". The transposition in the *Vulgata Clementina*, *mulierem sororem*, "have a woman as sister", finally makes this tendency apparent. Our textual criticism has enabled us to recover the original wording of Paul's statement and discover its meaning to be: the Lord granted the apostles and their fellow-workers the right to take their wives with them and to require for them too provision from the churches. Voluntary refraining from this right is possible and good, but it is a matter for the individual: the right, the freedom to marry, remains as granted by the Lord.

e. The question is now once again – and more pointedly than before – whether, against the right of all men including the apostles to a wife, guaranteed by God the creator and Christ the Lord, the prohibition by the Church as a human legislator can claim any validity at all. Is it not rather a void law from the outset? This all-decisive question must now receive our attention.

Chapter 4

Effects on the Prohibition of Marriage

Standing above all canon law are legal principles that derive from its character as being the law of believers: the Church – unlike the state, which is a community including non-believers – recognizes God as its direct lawgiver.

1. In his standard commentary, A. van Hove expresses this underlying principle in the following words: "Positive divine law (that is: law expressedly formulated in Holy Scipture, not simply deduced by reason as natural) and natural divine law are of themselves binding, even without any intervention from the Church. Positive divine law consists of the rights and duties of human beings as contained in the books of the Old and New Testament."[1] Many of us are used to thinking that divine law only imposes duties: the Ten Commandments, the duty to obey superiors in the Church and so on. Yet divine law confers rights too, not only imposes obligations. Since these rights are directly applicable to the individual in the Church, as van Hove says, it seems we can draw immediate consequences from the "right" of 1

---

1. A. van Hove, *Commentarium Lovaniense in Codicem Iuris Canonici* I/1, Prolegomena (Malines-Rome, 2nd ed. 1945) pp.48f: *"Ius divinum positivum et naturale per se est obligatorium, etiam absque ullo interventu Ecclesiae"*.

Corinthians 9:5. The new Code of Canon Law, too, contains quite a number of "rights" of the faithful (can. 224–231) which testify to the fresh sensibility of the church authorities to human rights in general. This provides a good starting point for the following considerations.

Van Hove continues: "Divine law is in force and is binding, even without its being set out by the Church in canon laws. No human law is superior to divine law."[2] And he proves it with regard to the old Code: "That the natural law (and the positive divine law) is in force in the Church, is expressedly said in can.6 n° 6" (of 1918),[3] to which canon. 199,1 of the new Code of 1983 corresponds. Indeed, canon law code has itself confirmed the validity of divine law by means of the old canon 6 which specifies that every "disciplinary law not contained in the codex (of 1918) is to be regarded as having no force, unless the law belongs to divine law, both the positive and the natural." Can. 199,1 of the new Code states that rights and duties of positive or natural divine law never expire.

From what we have discussed in the preceding chapter, it can firmly be asserted that the right or privilege of the apostles and their fellow-workers to take wives with them into their ministry is positive divine law contained in the scripture of the Old and New Testaments (Gen. 1:28; 2:18, 24 and 1 Cor. 9:5). Since in

---

2. Van Hove, *ibid.* p.51: *"Ius divinum viget et obligat, quin ab Ecclesia canonicis legibus proponatur. Nullum ius humanum contra ius divinum praevalet"*. See also K. Mörsdorf, *Kirchenrecht* I (Paderborn, 11th ed. 1964) p.21: "All divine law is directly applicable as canon law".
3. Van Hove, *ibid.* p.61: *"Ius naturale in Ecclesia vigere affirmat expresse can.6 n.6"*. Cf. his Commentary vol.I/2, *De legibus* (Malines-Rome, 1930) pp.75f.

our "apostolic" Church this right obviously also applies to the successors of the apostles and their fellow-workers, just as much as the rights of the apostle Peter apply to his successor, the pope, and the rights of the apostles to the bishops, we must conclude that the right to a female companion is in force, even according to the current canon law: see canon 199. Besides, the Preface to the Code says expressedly, with regard to bishops and their rights: "The office of bishops *together with the rights connected to it*, are of divine law."[4] Against this, no human law has priority or binding force. This means that the Church's prohibition of marriage for the successors of the apostles and their fellow-workers – for bishops and priests – is null and void.

It is like in the fairy-tale of The Emperor's new clothes: everyone thought he was dressed in gold and silk, but it took the simplicity of a child to cry out: "But look, he is not wearing anything at all!" And Christ praised the simplicity of children. So let us imitate their frankness: everyone has been afraid of the celibacy law; in fact, it does not exist at all. It is a *lex putativa*, an imagined law.

Therefore, every bishop and priest of the apostolic Church, as a successor of the apostles and their helpers, whether he has the charism of celibacy like Paul or not, has the "right" granted by the "Lord" (1 Cor. 9:14) "to be accompanied by a wife, as the other apostles and the brothers of the Lord and Cephas" actually were (1 Cor. 9:5).

Those who have the charism of celibacy will certainly, like Paul (1 Cor. 9:15), refrain from making use of this

---

4. See the *Preface* to the new Code, *principia approbata* no. 5: "*Officium episcoporum cum potestatibus adnexis est iuris divini*".

right. But those who do not have this charism of celibacy but rather that of marriage (1 Cor. 7:7), can, even under the provisions of the present law (can. 6 no.6 of 1917 and can. 199 of 1983) at any time and validly make use of this right which is established by the Lord Creator and the Lord Redeemer, that is, to take a wife with them as "helper" (Gen. 2:18; 1 Cor. 9:5), with "the right to food and drink" for her too, in other words, for her to be supported by the churches (1 Cor. 9:4).

2. In the secular state a law will remain in force until it has been declared null and void by the supreme or constitutional court.[5] In the same way, due to the collision between the rules of canon 199 on one hand and canons 277, 1087, 1394 of the 1983 CIC on the other, those priests who wish to marry in the church, will have to consider the following:

a. A canonical objection: the Lord bestowed on Peter the power that whatever he will bind on earth is to be bound in heaven also (Matt. 16:19: *hò eán*, whatever). The formula "whatever" obviously does not rule out erroneous prohibitions as well.[6] Yet "Peter" – or his successor – put canon 199 also into effect, and this makes the prohibitions of canons 277 and 1087 into doubtful laws. Such a doubtful law, however, does not oblige as is stated by another canon of the present code: "Laws, even those preventing something (for instance, marriage), are

---

5. Cf. H. Weinkauff, "Widerstandsrecht", in *Staatslexikon* 8 (Freiburg, 1963) p.682.
6. From the text of the New Testament, it is not quite clear what is meant by "bind" and loosen". In rabinic usage it means both "to declare to be allowed or forbidden" and "ban and lift a ban': see A. Vögtle on the word in: LThK, 2nd ed., I, 480.

not binding, if there is any doubt as to their validity" (can. 14 CIC).[7]" On the other hand, "the highest ecclesiastical authority" has reserved to itself the competence "to declare authentically, when divine law forbids or dissolves a marriage", according to canon 1075 §1. This could be interpretetd as applying also in the inverse sense that divine law does not actually bring about separation but validity of a marriage.

Besides, the Council of Trent has stated that it is the duty of the doctrinal authority, the *magisterium*, and not of science, to confirm that, in 1 Corinthians 9:5, a divinely sanctioned right of the apostles and their helpers is expressed.[8]

These rules serve the stability of law and peace, which were also of high value for Paul (1 Cor. 14:33: "God is not a God of disorder but of peace"). This means that any doubtful law has first to be officially repealed, before it can be simply disregarded. The personal endeavours of the present writer to obtain a decision from the Holy See about the divine law in 1 Corinthians 9:5 ended with the answer that it "does not wish to decide" (21 August 1987), though the Secretariat of State admitted in a letter dated 2 December 1986 (N° 187.480) that "the apostles obviously were married". To the objection that St Paul does not speak only of facts but of "rights" the secretariat gave no response.

b. A moral objection: moral theology puts forward the principle: "A law which is morally or physically *impossible*, is not binding."[9] A priest who with increasing

---

7. Can.14 CIC: *"Leges, etiam irritantes et inhabilitantes, in dubio iuris non urgent"*.
8. DS 1507.
9. B. Häring, *Das Gesetz Christi* I (Freiburg, 6th ed. 1961) pp.309, 320.

certainty discovers that he does not have the charism of
celibacy will in his conscience certainly be justified in
entering into marriage, since he finds himself facing an
impossible law. Since, however, the possibility of his
being dispensed from the celibacy law exists,[10] and,
furthermore, since marriage also affects the civil realm
outside the Church, "marriage in conscience" will, it is
true, often be the only way open, but hardly the best way
to choose. The rule: *Lex non obligat cum gravi incommodo*
(a law does not oblige, if it involves grave inconven-
ience) may "only be made use of after serious consideration of the law's inner nature and of the offence which
may perhaps result from its not being followed".[11]

Those who draw attention to the *injustice* of the law
are in a similar case. The rule applies to them too:
"Unjust laws do not, as such, bind the conscience. But
the conscience is bound to the extent demanded by
general order, by the avoidance of offence, protection
from great inner unrest or from heavy punishment from
outside."[12] For the sake of peace among Christians, Paul
says to the Corinthians, concerning their freedom to eat
heathen sacrificial meat: "Take care lest this liberty of
yours somehow becomes a stumbling-block to the
weak" (1 Cor. 8:9). In the same way as the freedom of the
strong in Corinth to eat the meat from the heathen

---

10. The term "laicisation" should never be adopted for this measure,
and is, in fact, no longer used by the Vatican authorities, because it is
banned by Trent: "If someone says that a priest who was once priest
can turn to be a lay person again, he shall be excluded", "*si quis
dixerit. . eum, qui semel sacerdos fuit, laicum rursus fieri posse, anathema
sit*" (DS 1774). That is why the new Code speaks only of the "loss of
the clerical state", but not of the state in which the dispensed priest
arrives! (can. 292).
11. Mörsdorf, *Kirchenrecht* I, p.105.
12. Häring, *Das Gesetz Christi* I, p.310.

temples, was – out of love – not to be made use of, until all had *realized* that the idols do not exist, in the same way nowadays the freedom of the apostles' successors and their helpers to take wives with them ought not – out of love – to be made use of, until the time when all are convinced of the celibacy law's being null and void, and until this fact is officially determined. Exceptions to this rule are possible by way of equity (*epikia*).[13]

c. A dogmatic objection: the Council of Trent, in canon 9 of the 24th session, condemned the view, "all clerics who have received the holy orders and members of religious orders who have vowed celibacy, may marry, if they realize they do not have the gift of chastity, and the marriage entered to is valid without any let from canon law".[14] Since what is at stake is the valid coming into being of the sacrament of marriage, which the Church has the power to administer, dogmatic matter is at least touched upon here. Earlier, in chapter 2, we saw that canon 9 of Trent sought to affirm the council fathers' competence concerning marriage.[15] But it was not till Vatican I that the criteria on what matters can be defined infallibly by the Church were stated: "With faith owed to God and the Catholic Church all is to be believed that the written or handed down word of God contains and what the Church in its solemn or ordinary magisterium

---

13. On equity (*epikia*) cf. Mörsdorf I, pp.102–5, 115, especially 103: "It will not cease to apply to the inhibiting laws (as the marriage obstacle is), as well".
14. DS 1809; see above, ch.2, n.17.
15. See above, ch.2, n.18.

proposes as to be believed as truth revealed by God".[16]
Nobody will say that "canon law", including that on
celibacy, is revealed by God, or that it is contained in the
written or handed down word of God. Church law is not
definable. Trent could not define the infallibility of a
disciplinary law which *per definitionem* is fallible. Trent
could not make dogma out of discipline.

d. A further dogmatic objection: In another Tridentine
decree, canon 4 of the same 24th session, the opinion is
banned "that the Church was wrong in enunciating
marital impediments which dissolve marriages" (*impedimenta dirimentia*).[17] In the case of the celibacy law
under discussion, this is a historical problem, since it is
not unequivocally clear whether the Second Lateran
Council of 1139 validly drew up the "dissolving" marital
impediment of ordination (and not rather, as before, a
prohibiting one which did not affect the validity of
priests' marriages). An "*ecclesiastica regula*", a church
ruling on human law, as the law of 1139 qualifies itself,
can, indeed, according to our understanding and that of
its time, never annul "*ius divinum*", divine law, which the
human right to marry is. That the legislator himself was
not very sure about his own law can be deduced from
the wording of canon 7 of 1139: the synod members say
only with regard to marriages of priests: "We *hold* such a
union, obviously contracted in contrast to the rule of the

---

16. DS 3012: "*Fide divina et catholica ea omnia credenda sunt, quae in verbo
Dei scripto vel tradito continentur et ab Ecclesia sive sollemni iudicio sive
ordinario et universali magisterio tamquam divinitus revelata credenda
proponuntur*". Cf. the defintion of papal and ecclesiastical infallibility
solely on matters of "faith and morals": DS 3073.
17. DS 1804.

Church, not to be a marriage".[18] At the Synod of Pisa four years earlier (1135), which is not regarded as a general council, the same canon had been formulated in almost the same words, except for the unambiguous legislative term: "We *determine* that such a union is no marriage".[19] If the general council of 1139 did not make use of this formula, this was obviously deliberate and permits the conclusion that the council had some doubts about its power to abrogate a fundamental right belonging to the clergy. Otherwise it would have adopted the technical language of a lawgiver. In fact, the council did not declare the *nullity* of priests' marriages but its *opinion* about this issue, and that on grounds that rule out infallibility, firstly because reference to a "rule of the church" has nothing to do with *ius divinum* and just as little with faith or morals; secondly because the purpose "to spread purity among the clergy",[20] is an erroneous motive. As regards canon 7 of 1139, we are faced with a purely disciplinary canon; this is why it does not appear in Denzinger. There is no definable matter in it, so it cannot have been declared infallible by canon 4 of the 24th session of Trent. A doubt as to the legal force of canon 7 of 1139 remains possible.

The conclusion to be drawn is that it remains a fact that, for the successors of the apostles and their helpers, the right to marry *exists* in the realm of conscience. Nevertheless, there is a requirement of love not to make

---

18. Conc. Oec. Decr., p.175: "*Huiusmodi namque copulationem, quam contra ecclesiasticam regulam constat esse contractam, matrimonium non esse censemus*".

19. J.D. Mansi, *Sacrorum conciliorum nova et amplissima collectio* 21, 489, quoted by Denzler I,83: "*Huiusmodi namque copulationem.. matrimonium non esse sancimus*".

20. See above, ch.2, n.13.

use of this right in the public forum, before an official
statement has been made by the responsible authority
that the law in conflict with this right is void. *Epikia*,
however, remains possible.

3. Up to this point, we have deduced the invalidity of the
celibacy law from the continued existence of the special
apostolic right to take a wife as a companion. This is
indeed the strongest argument against a special *prohibition* of the same by the church authorities. Divine law is
above church law. But the Church has not yet confirmed
that it is divine law. However, besides its conflict with
this special *apostolic* right, the invalidity of the prohibition can also be deduced from the universal *human right*
to marry, which was expressedly recognized and stated
by Pope Leo XIII. For priests remain human beings and
cannot forfeit their natural God-given right to marry
through a man-made law. Pope Leo XIII says exactly that
in a sentence of the celebrated encyclical *Rerum Novarum*,
which Pius XI quoted in his no less famous encyclical
Casti connubii: "No human law can take away from man
the original human right to marry."[21] It is difficult to
understand how the law on celibacy, which tries to do
just this, could escape the attention of these two popes.
The Church has always called the celibacy law "human
law", "*ecclesiastica regula*" (Lateran II), "*lex ecclesiastica*"
(Trent), "ecclesiastical law" (Mörsdorf),[22] and it does
precisely what Leo XIII declares to be impossible: it
prohibits marriage right up to canon 132 of 1918 and the
current canons 277 and 1087 of 1983. These laws do not

---

21. AAS 22 (1930) p.542: "*Ius coniugii naturale et primigenum. . homini
adimere lex hominum nulla potest*".
22. Mörsdorf, *Kirchenrecht* I, p.261.

counsel remaining unmarried; nor do they select the charismatics of celibacy; they simply prevent priests from marrying or from making use of marital rights. Leo XIII declares such laws unable to take away the natural right to marry: Therefore they are *nullae*, invalid, according to the papal statement.

a. The Synod of Elvira (324) probably, if it is really to be interpreted in this way, but certainly Pope Siricius (385) and the council of Carthage (401), *forbade* all bishops, priests and deacons, any longer to fulfil their marital duties to their wives, which Paul in 1 Corinthians 7:3–5 enjoined as strictly incumbent on the conscience. So, the law directly contradicts revelation; it also contradicts the sentence of Leo XIII's ruling that no human law can interfere with or take away the natural right to marry: it is invalid.

b. The Second Lateran Council asserted that it did not regard marriage entered into by clergy as marriage, and that those who had been married were to be separated.[23] The decree says that priests had infringed a *propositum*, an intention or a promise of their own making (more honestly, the Roman edition has: they have broken the law, *praeceptum*). In fact, it is certain that it was not the spontaneous abstinence of priests from their right to marry that led to the law, but the other way round: the legislators were seeking to elicit abstinence, and it was precisely in this that they failed before they *took away*

---

23. Conc. Oec. Decr. 175: "*Statuimus, quatenus, qui sanctum transgredientes propositum uxores sibi copulare praesumpserint, separentur, huiusmodi namque copulationem. . matrimonium non esse censemus*". Roman edition of the ecumenical councils (1608–12, COD *ibid*.): instead of "*propositum*" read "*praeceptum*".

from priests their right to marry, which was a right
tolerated up to this point.[24] The very fact that, in spite of
all the preceding laws, priests were still marrying in 1139
and then were to be forcibly separated by a new law,
proves that there was not much of liberty or personal
intention in priests' obedience to the laws. We have
already seen that this was due to the lack of the "special
charism" which is necessary for voluntary abstinence,
and due to the presence of the "other charism" of
marriage (1 Cor. 7:7). At that time, however, neither the
law-makers nor those subjected to it were aware of the
need for the charism. In any case, the law intruded into
existing and valid marriages (as they were held to be up
to this time): according to revealed law, this was
impossible, as all knew, see Matthew 19:6: "What God
has joined together, let no man put asunder". The
motives were clear: They wanted to keep priests from
marriage because it was regarded as something "impure".[25] But even inasmuch as the law sought to prevent
priests from marrying in the future, without considering
their voluntary abstaining – as is the case with the
marital impediment of solemn vows, which the corresponding law (can. 1088) only confirms – the law-makers
clearly exceeded their competence, according to Leo
XIII's ruling, because the human right to marry cannot
be taken away from priests who do not voluntarily give
it up. So, the law of 1139 is null and void.

---

24. On a Whitsunday around 1090, the archdeacon of Coutances,
surrounded by his wife and children and all the married clergy of the
town, protested against the monk Bernard of Tiron who preached the
ideas of Pope Gregory VII: "Why do you preach to the living, whilst
you are a monk and dead to the world?": Migne, PL 172, 1397–9; see
J.-L. Declais, *Réponse* (above, ch.2, n.31).
25. See above, ch.2, n.13.

c. Canon 132 of the 1918 Code, taken together with canon 1072, says that the higher clergy "are *prevented* from marrying" by a general rule stemming from their ordination, independently from their personal renunciation.[26] The motives were the same as in 1139: unchastity is a sacrilege.[27] Any law that takes away the right to marry is void: this applies equally to canons 132 and 1072 of 1918. Soon after 1918, however, as a consequence of the increasing consciousness of universal human rights, it was noticed that in the wording of the law no consideration was taken of personal renunciation by the individual under obligation. Therefore, since 1930, the highest authority in the Church has demanded the taking of the so-called "free-will-oath".[28] In doing so, this authority has admitted that up till then the law had no foundation in expressed personal renunciation by the individual; so, it was invalid. The Church itself was a forerunner in the recognition of inalienable human rights,[29] which spread from the American Declaration of Independence of 1776 and by way of the French Constitution of 1789, for since the Middle Ages it had elaborated the idea of natural law. An instance of this is precisely Leo XIII's ruling on the *"ius coniugii naturale"*. Consequently, the law-makers of 1918 were to be made answerable for their error even according to the stan-

---

26. Can. 132 CIC/1918: *"Clerici in maioribus ordinibus constituti a nuptiis arcentur. . "*. Can. 1072: *"Invalide matrimonium attentant clerici in maioribus constituti"*.
27. See above, ch.2, p. 61.
28. AAS 23 (1931), p.127. Since 15 Aug. 1972, because of Paul's VI *Motu Proprio*, a personal public *Consecratio*, replacing the oath, is required: *Pontificale Romanum* (Rome, 1972), pp.29f; AAS 64 (1972), p.539.
29. Cf. LThK, 2nd ed., VII, 297.

dards then applicable. The law of 1918 was no valid law.

Only one question remans: whether the free-will oath of 1930 – replaced since 1972 by public consecration during the ordination ceremonies – has changed anything. By that oath, however, the ordination candidate did not, in the first place, affirm that he was spontaneously giving up a right, but rather his knowledge of the law and his readiness to obey it: "Especially I declare well to have realized the significance of the celibacy law, and I promise willingly to obey it and with God's help to observe it wholly unto my last day."[30] Since 1972 the ordination rite requires an answer to the question: "Will you observe celibacy?" What is primary is the law's demand which the candidate has only to obey. In 1930 too, the presence of the *charism* in the candidate was not asked about, because even at that time no account of the need for it had yet been drawn up; it was asked from a purely legal motivation whether the candidate knew the celibacy law and would willingly fulfill it. Neither does the free-will oath take notice of a prior spontaneous renunciation by each individual whereby he has waived the exercise of his right to marry; this waiver would alone, perhaps, justify a legal sanction, as is done with the vows of religious orders. In no way, however, would the renunciation justify the heavy penal sanctions of canon 2388 of 1918 or canon 1394 of 1983, dealing with a

---

30. AAS 23 (1931), p.127: *"Praecipue quae caelibatus lex importet, clare me percipere ostendo, eamque libenter explere atque integre servare usque ad extremum Deo adiuvante firmiter statuo"*. In the ordination rites, since 1972 candidates are asked:*"Vultis. . caelibatum. . custodire?"*

priest who revokes his waiver.[31] In fact, all that the oath is about, is the law and obedience to it.

So, the question remains whether this compulsory law in itself is justified. And precisely the right of the church authority to demand from each and every candidate for the priesthood such a renunciation needs to be discussed. A renunciation which is demanded is, by its nature, no free renunciation.[32] Rather, it is obedience to an "imposed obligation" – thus the language even of Vatican II[33] – which is "not indeed demanded by the

---

31. Cf. H.U. Wili, *Zur Zölibatspflicht der Weltkleriker im katholischen Kirchenrecht*: Theologische Berichte 4 (Cologne-Einsiedeln, 1974) pp.213–24, 230 n.180.

32. The old dispute as to whether the celibate state rests on an implicit vow or on canon law – vow-theory and law-theory – even after the Church's requirement of the free-will oath has not been buried but rekindled afresh by Pius XII's encyclical *Sacra virginitas* (AAS 46, 1954, 161–91). At that time, W. Bertrams, a canonist teaching in Rome, expressed the view that the law incorporates the obligation to take a vow, in several articles: *Periodica de re morali canonica liturgica* 44 (1955) 139–74; 50 (1961) 204–11; *Geist und Leben* 28 (1955) 95–104, as well as in a book: *Der Zölibat des Priesters* (Würzburg, 2nd ed. 1962). Since it is a contradiction in itself to demand by law the taking of a spontaneous vow which, according to Bertrams too, can only be taken *"voluntate omnino libera"* (*Periodica* 44,148), there have been firm rebuttals of his view from other canon law professors such as K. Mörsdorf in *Kirchenrecht* I (Paderborn, 9th ed. 1959) pp.271f, B. Häring, *Das Gesetz Christi* III (Freiburg, 6th ed. 1961) p.397; J. Lederer, in: *Archiv für katholisches Kirchenrecht* 129 (Mainz, 1959f) 668f. Therefore, the prevailing opinion can be seen to be that the celibacy of the priest rests on canon law, not on a vow. We are thus confirmed in our statement that a vow is not the same as obedience to a law, even if the latter is voluntary. See E. Schillebeeckx, *Der Amtszölibat* (Düsseldorf, 1967) p.54: "The fact that, right up to the present, the polemic has continued as to whether or not ordination of priests encompasses an (at least implicit) vow of celibacy, points to the fact that theology has somehow come to a standstill due to an unsolved problem."

33. PO 16, see above, ch.2, n.52; for the following, n. 43.

very nature of the priesthood". Therefore it cannot be demanded from every priest as perhaps can other obligations of his calling. The historical sequence was this: first came the prohibition for Latin priests to marry; then subsequent legitimation was sought by "voluntary obedience" and an "oath of free will"; but the prohibition remained in existence as such; its place was not taken by the Church's acceptance of the spontaneous renunciation of the natural right, as is the case when a vow is taken in religious orders. A prohibition which is, in itself, contrary to divine law, cannot be made legitimate by individuals subjected to it; this could only be done by God.

The marriage impediment of orders contained in canon 132 (1918) and canon. 277 or 1080 (1983), which is in itself contrary to natural law, is and remains invalid, if we follow Leo XIII, despite the free-will oath. That also applies to the rite prescribed since 1972: celibacy remains an *"obligatio"*, not a spontaneous vow.

4. To sum up: this human, natural right to marry proclaimed by Pope Leo XIII, has moreover been vindicated, as stated above, by the apostle Paul for the apostles and their fellow-workers also, as a special apostolic right of office, and has thus been given a still higher sanction by scripture (1 Cor. 9:4–6, in combination with the right to being provided for by the communities). Neither *ius divinum naturale* nor *ius divinum positivum* can be rescinded by the Church (can. 199 CIC/1983). Therefore the law of canon 277 is null and void.

Furthermore, it is invalid also on account of its untenable "purity" motivation which was at its origin and can be traced down to canon 132 of 1918 and to Pope Paul VI.

To this we must add the lack of binding force for those priests who do not have the charism, since they are being put under an obligation to do something which is impossible for them without a charism.

A further reason for the law's invalidity is the fact that it conflicts with the axiom of equality: equal matters have to be treated equally in the East and West of the Catholic Church.

The law of compulsory celibacy is against human rights, against apostolic rights in scripture, against the inamenability of charisms, against the holiness of marriage (in its original motivation), against the requirements of equality in the rules of admission to priesthood. So there are at least five grounds of invalidity which support and complement each other. The law is null and void. It must be officially repealed .

5. With regard to the pastoral situation, it must be stated that the celibacy law nowadays represents a similar barrier to the spread of the Kingdom of God, as, at the time of the apostle Paul, did the Old Testament food laws: on the one hand, from 1964 on, more than 80.000 priests have been forced to give up their ministry in order to be able to marry, and vocations to a celibate priesthood are continually and massively decreasing. On the other hand, a constantly growing number of theology students is pressing into vocations within the Church, but outside the ordained priesthood: what prevents them from wishing to be ordained is compulsory celibacy. The Church is strangling itself through too tough a fidelity to (human!) traditions.

In Paul's times, the "uncleanness" of certain foods was

no longer covered by the will of God (Mark 7:15). Peter himself knew about this (Acts 10:9–16). Nevertheless, Paul had to "resist" Peter in order to make him realize the freedom Christ had brought us (Gal. 2:11–14).

In our times, the "uncleanness" of sexual acts is no longer covered by the will of God; this fact has long since been available to everyone from the words of the Lord in Mark 7:14–23 and the other passages of scripture on the holiness of marriage and self-surrender in marriage (1 Thess. 4:4; 1 Pet. 3:7; Heb. 13:4 and Eph. 5:22–32). What is created "good" (Gen 1:31) cannot become through legitimate use "bad" and unclean in the moral sense. This is what the criticism from the East indicated in the 51st Apostolic Canon.[34] It is said, with even harsher criticism, by Paul or his disciple in 1 Timothy 4:1–4, in regard to "forbidding marriage", which he qualifies as the "doctrine of demons": "Everything created by God is good, and nothing is to be rejected if it is received with thanksgiving". Yet, in fact, celibacy as the compulsory state of Roman Catholic priests, came into being as a "prohibition of the rights of marriage". We should take our leave from this prohibition. Vatican II made a promising start in this direction by weeding out its motivation and by affirming that a married priest too can love God with an undivided heart. "Those unable to marry for the sake of the Kingdom of Heaven, who make *themselves* unable to marry" (Matt. 19:11f), *without* a law preventing marriage, there will always be, since we can trust the words of the Lord.

---

34. See above, ch.2, n.3.

Chapter 5

Is the Charism of Celibacy Suitable as a Mandatory Condition of Admission to the Priesthood?

Regardless of whether celibacy is at present (*de lege lata*) a mandatory condition of admission, which, on the evidence of current laws, is not the case, we need – on account of the current interpretation by many a bishop[1] – to consider the possibility that church authorities could at some time (*de lege ferenda*) expressedly make the presence of the charism of celibacy a criterion of selection or condition of admission to the priestly ministry.

That present-day legislation already operates as such a condition of admission has no significance for the existing laws, because they were promulgated with a

---

1. For instance the German bishops, see Joseph Kardinal Höffner, "Uber den Zölibat der Priester, Um des Himmelreiches willen. Zehn Thesen", in *Themen und Thesen* 1 (Cologne, 6th ed. 1975, reprinted to 1986) p.15: "The bishop is only then entitled to exercise the imposition of hands on a deacon for his priestly ordination when the deacon, after serious and sober consideration, has arrived at the sincere conviction that the Lord has given him the dual gift of grace: the call to priesthood and the call to celibacy for the sake of the Kingdom of Heaven". He quotes, *ibid.* p.16, the *Statement of German bishops on the celibacy of priests*, dated 19 Feb. 1970: "The fact that celibacy for the sake of the Kingdom of Heaven is a gift of God's grace does not prevent it from being made a criterion of selection for priestly service". It would be interesting to know the reasons for this unproven assertion by the bishops. Nor do we get any, for the same assertion, by Alvaro del Portillo, see above, ch.2, n.61.

different intention, as illustrated in the preceding chapters. But how would we judge the laws if they expressedly stated that only those who are entitled to presume that they have received the charism of celibacy are to be admitted to the priesthood of the Latin, Western Church? So far not even Vatican Council II has laid down any condition of admission in *Presbyterorum Ordinis 16* – nor does the new canon 277 of the 1983 CIC do so – but it holds fast to the old *obligation* of restraint "imposed" on those ordained. However, the Council was aware that celibacy can be achieved only through the charism, which is why it exhorts priests to try to gain possession of the charism for themselves by prayer. This shows the weakness of the lawgivers' position.

What, then, would there be to be said, from a theological and a canonical viewpoint, if the charism were to be unequivocally laid down as a criterion of selection for the Latin priesthood?

The church authorities have unambiguously declared themselves bound to the priority of divine law in the Church, in canon. 6 no. 6 (1918) and in the Preface and canon. 199 (1983).[2] Hence, it would not go against the *"sentire cum ecclesia"* if, having drawn attention to this higher law, the power so to legislate were to be denied to church leaders. Divine law is in force and cannot be neglected. What follows gives four reasons for the limitation of the legislative power of the Church in this point.

1. *God calls Married Persons to the Priesthood*

According to the New Testament and prevailing theological teaching, both a divine and the Church's call

---

2. See above, ch.4, nn.2–4.

are necessary for priestly vocation: Jesus chooses as apostles "those whom *he* desired" (Mark 3:13). He sends the apostles, and through them their successors, to all peoples (Matt. 28:19). Paul says to the elders gathered together in Ephesus at his farewell: "The *Holy Spirit* has made you bishops over your flocks" (Acts 20:28),[3] although it was he himself who had appointed them and administered the laying on of hands to them (Acts 14:23). Similarly twofold, the Pauline school says in 1 Timothy 4:14: "Do not neglect the charism (of ministry!) you have, which was given you by prophetic utterance[4] when the elders laid their hands upon you,"[5] and in 2 Timothy 1:6: "Rekindle the gift of God (for ministry!) that is within you through the laying on of my hands."[6] The letter to

---

3. Cf. K. Kertelge, *Gemeinde und Amt im Neuen Testament* (Community and office in the New Testament) (Munich, 1972) p.102, on Acts 20:28: "The presbyterate as a Christian office is not founded on the fact of selection or appointment of the individual office-holders by the church, but on the authority of Jesus. Luke also understands the office of elder in this sense as an office empowered by the Spirit (Acts 20:28). Here, the specifically Christian quality of this office is expressed in a theologically adequate manner". See *ibid.* p.11 on Mark 3:13–19, and p.22 on Matt. 29:19.

4. See N. Brox, *Die Pastoralbriefe*: RNT 7,2 (Regensburg, 4th ed. 1969) pp.118, 180, with H. von Campenhausen: "This was an 'inspired election'". H. Schlier, *Die Zeit der Kirche* (The Era of the Church) (Freiburg, 1956) p.137: "An indication of prophets is found in 1 Tim 1:18 and 4:14. They indicated Timothy as the right person to attain to the office of bishop, and in this way, in accordance with the early Christian understanding, exercised the *iudicium dei* (!) which was recognized by Paul".

5. Cf. Brox p.182: "The laying on of hands itself is reserved to the superior office: that is, the presbyterium (1 Tim. 4:14), the apostle (2 Tim. 1:6), or Timothy (1 Tim. 5:22)". Kertelge pp.146, 148: "The office is passed on through the laying on of hands".

6. Brox p. 228 briefly summarizes the two elements: "He summons to awaken the charisma (gift of grace) received through the laying on of hands (ordination), that is the 'charisma of grace for office'".

the Hebrews refers only to the divine calling: "No one takes this honour on himself, but each one is called by God, as Aaron was" (5:4).[7]

Accordingly, the function of the Church's call is seen in later theological and conciliar teaching as being officially to establish the presence of a divine calling, and the appointment of the candidate to his office in the Church: "Those have to be considered as called by God, who are called by the legitimate ministers of the church."[8]

Now it is an indisputable fact that God calls married men to the priesthood as well as celibates. This knowledge is based on the New Testament witness (Mark 1:30; 1 Cor. 9:5; 1 Tim. 3:2, 12) and on the uninterrupted tradition of the Eastern Churches, including the Catholic ones,[9] as well as on the dispensations granted by popes to converted married clergy in the West since the time of Pius XII. All these married men have been accepted by the Church. Both elements came together in their calling to the ministry. Then we must ask where the Latin church finds the justification for expressedly selecting only unmarried men, charismatics of celibacy for the

---

7. Cf. e.g. H. Strathmann, *Der Brief an die Hebräer*: NTD 9 (Göttingen, 1953), pp.96, 98: "The basic condition for the office of (high) priest is: the divine calling as against human pretension".

8. *Catechismus Romanus* P.II cap.7 n.3: "*Nec enim quisquam sibi sumat honorem, sed qui vocatur a Deo tamquam Aaron. Vocati autem a Deo dicuntur, qui a legitimis ecclesiae ministris vocantur*". Vatican II in *Optatam Totius* speaks of "lawful ministers of the Church (to whom God) confides the work of calling proven candidates whose fitness has been acknowledged" (Abbott, p.440): "*divinitus electos, idoneitate agnita, comprobatos vocent et consecrent*".

9. Vatican II refers to both of them in PO 16b, Abbott, p.565. Cf. also the famous speech by the late Patriarch Maximos IV Saigh, not delivered in the council but distributed later by the Press: "Priestertum, Zölibat und Ehe in der Ostkirche" in *Der Seelsorger* (Vienna) 37 (1967) 302–6.

ministry? It is true that the individual *candidate* who, as a married man, would like to become a priest, does not have the *right* of admission to the priesthood; the decision as to admission is reserved to the "local bishop's determination" (can. 1025 and 1029, 1983). Yet it is *God's right* to choose whom he wants that is at stake. The church authorities are not wholly free as to general principles when setting out the conditions of admission: they are bound to the norms of the divine right laid down in holy scripture. If it is firmly established in scripture and tradition that God's call to priestly ministry also goes out to married men, then the leadership of the Latin Church is actually debarred from refusing in general and on principle all those who are married. The church law itself calls such a behaviour a *"nefas"*, a sacrilege, an offence "against all divine law":[10] "It is a sacrilege to alienate anyone from the priesthood who is canonically suited to it".

Canon 1026 speaks of "canonically suitable". Anyone who would have been suited at the time of the early Church and is suited in the Church of the East cannot be unsuited in the West. If, in fact, married men, in general and on principle, according to the evidence of early times and Eastern parts of the Church, are suitable both in God's eyes and in the view of the church authorities, the Latin authorities cannot for their part declare them unsuitable: *Contra factum non valet argumentum.* If the Church authorities of the West expressedly refuse a

---

10. Can. 1026 CIC/1983. Cf. H. Jone, *Gesetzbuch der lateinischen Kirche* II (Paderborn, 2nd ed. 1952) p.72 on can. 817 CIC/1918. *Ibid.* p.193 on can. 971 CIC/1918, the new can. 1026: "It is a sacrilege to force anyone to take holy orders. It is likewise a sacrilege to turn someone, suitable as a candidate in accordance with church requirements, away from holy orders".

whole category of men as possibly chosen by God for the priesthood, they commit the *nefas* castigated by canon 1026. Since even the High Priests of the Old Covenant refrained from impeding the work of the apostles, as in the words of Gamaliel: "Leave these men alone. . you might find yourselves fighting against God!" (Acts 5:38f), we may hope that the good shepherds of the Church will refrain from impeding the work of married priests, if they are faced with the awkward consequence: "you might find yourselves fighting against God".

2. *The Apostles ordained Married Men*

Establishing the charism of celibacy as a condition of admission to the priesthood, would, furthermore, offend against the customs and rules of the apostles, the *ius apostolicum*. According to 1 Corinthians 9:5; 1 Timothy 3:2, 12 and Titus 1:6 the apostles admitted married men to the priesthood as a matter of course. The *ius apostolicum*, however, has a normative significance in the Apostolic Church for the *ius mere ecclesiasticum*.[11] It is located between the *ius divinum* and the *ius humanum* of the Church, because it is determined by the recipients of revelation themselves. Hence, the early Church and the Eastern Churches[12] again and again invoke "the apostolic canons". In the Latin Church too, the apostolic right of the *Privilegium Paulinum* (1 Cor 7:5ff) for instance, became, owing to its high rank, *ius ecclesiasticum*: canon 1143 (1983). What applies to Paul's order in matters of divorce on grounds of faith consequently applies also to

11. See A. van Hove, *Commentarium in CIC I,1, Prolegomena* (Malines-Rome, 2nd ed. 1945) pp.49f: *"In Scriptura Novi Testamenti sunt etiam (iura, p.49, et) praecepta iuris mere apostolici, non divini"*.
12. Cf. the Trullan synod of 692, see above ch.2, n.7.

Paul's regulations for the laying on of hands in the Pastoral Letters: they are normative for the Church. His temporary rule that women were to appear veiled at church services (1 Cor. 11:1–15) cannot be argued against this, since this was a rule conditioned by its time and capable being annulled: Paul himself expressly designates it as a "custom" or as a "practice" he follows with some communities (1 Cor. 11:16), not as a "right" as in 1 Corinthians 9:5.

In all other cases, the "Catholic and Apostolic Church" is always proud to trace its essential basis back to the apostolic origin. In this case, it has not upheld the origins but distanced itself from these, and would do so still further, if it were to lay down the charism of celibacy as a condition of admission to the priesthood.

3. *The Charism of Celibacy is given to only a Few*

Here we must repeat what has been said earlier. When Jesus warned: "Not all men are capable of making this real" (Matt. 19:11), he did not exclude priests from his warning. On the contrary: the apostles, his first future "priests", were first addressed: not all of you are capable![13] Nowhere does Jesus establish a special connection to the priesthood. Admittedly, the motivation for the *eunuchía*, namely "unmarried for the sake of the Kingdom of Heaven" (Matt. 19:12), indicates that this charism is most suitable for the service of the Kingdom. Yet it is in no way said that all those whom the Lord calls to this service will be equipped with the charism. His "wise saying" states only: "There *are* those unable to marry for the sake of the Kingdom of Heaven". This can refer to clergy and laity, to men and women, religious

---

13. See above, ch.1, esp.n.1; ch.2, last par.

and secular faithful. And, indeed, there are relatively few of them, just as there are few unable to marry because of defect from birth or as a result of an operation. To declare these few, who have a special grace, to be *alone* suitable for an office which is *generally* necessary for the survival of the Church at all times and in all places, would be a contradiction in itself and to disobey the Lord's warning: what is necessary in general – "elders in every city" (Acts 14:23) – cannot be tied to conditions which *per definitionem Domini* "not all can realize". Besides, it would mean refusing married men and thus rebelling against God's choice of these, too.

4. *Every Minister may* iure divino *take a Wife with Him*

As shown in chapter 3, all candidates for church office and even office-holders have the divine right to be accompanied by a wife.[14] Confronted with this divine right, any canon law condition of admission, that is a law *iuris mere ecclesiastici et humani* that accepts celibates only, remains *per se* legally ineffective, because the lower law gives way to the higher. The apostles' claim to a right to be accompanied in their work by a wife and to be supported with her by the communities is traced back by Paul to the Lord, that is to say to *ius divinum* (1 Cor. 9:4–5, 14). Yet such a claim, because it is of an "inviolable" nature,[15] has to be "acknowledged in such a

---

14. Cf. A. van Hove, *Commentarium in CIC* I,1, p.49: "Ius divinum positivum, a Deo libere et directe constitutum, constat iuribus (!) et officiis hominum, quae non defluunt ex ipsa eorum natura".

15. In *Dignitatis humanae* (DH) 1, Vatican II speaks of *"inviolabilibus humanae personae iuribus"*. In his commentary, P. Pavan says on this point (LThK Council II, 713): "The popes have emphasized ever more clearly the dignity of the human individual whom they have proclaimed as the holder of indestructable rights in the economic, political and *religious* realm".

way that it becomes (canon) law".[16] In other words, it cannot be abrogated but has to be incorporated into the Code.

There is but one question remaining, namely whether church authority can demand from candidates for the priesthood voluntary denial of exercising this right. This is probably what Pope Paul VI had in mind when requiring a public *consecratio*.[17] He obviously wanted to settle the old dispute about the foundation of celibacy, whether in law or in vow, by basing it expressedly on voluntary denial.[18] Here, too, the problems overlap: as the Lord declares and as Vatican II finally recognizes,[19] abstention from marriage can be achieved only by virtue of the charism. If the public promise "to observe celibacy" were meant to elicit voluntary abstention from the divine right to marry, then it would, for those who have not received the charism of celibacy, be requiring something impossible, and accordingly not binding.[20] However, should the required promise to remain celibate signify the selection of those who are enabled to remain unmarried only, then this selective aim would be affected by the arguments already adduced, namely that the Latin hierarchy calls fewer priests into service in the Western Church than God himself does and the Eastern

---

16. So says the Council with reference to the freedom of religion, DH 2b: "This right of the human person. . is to be recognized in the constitutional law whereby society is governed. Thus it is to become civil right". The same applies to the individual's rights within the Church: they must become canon law.
17. AAS 64 (1972) 539, see above, ch.4, n.28.
18. See above, ch.4, n.32. Cf. Wili, *Zur Zölibatspflicht*, p.223.
19. PO 16f, n.194.
20. See above, ch.2, n.64.

Church accepts, a process which canon law describes in canon 1026 as *nefas*.

If the unattainability of charismatic celibacy is taken seriously, there is no possibility of basing priestly celibacy on voluntary denial of human rights. Mere goodwill is not enough to enact this waiver; a charism is needed, one which is not given to everyone (Matt. 19:11).

Furthermore, for the same reason the Church hierarchy cannot select only those few favoured by God with a double charism, that of ministry and that of celibacy: this would interfere with God's rights.

In fact, the power so to legislate has to be denied to church leaders. Whichever way the law is interpreted, it remains untenable and unimprovable.

A civil lawgiver would be unable to demand abstention from exercise of the marriage right, since human basic rights are of a higher order than any kind of civil requirements to abstain, once laid down in some states for policemen or women teachers.[21] Such a law would be invalid as being against good morals (*contra bonos mores*) and the constitution. Besides, the Church's lawgivers cannot demand it for another reason: they know the need for the charism of celibacy, which is not at their disposal nor at that of those subject to them. The fact that God has not coupled the charism of celibacy to the

---

21. According to German jurisprudence and legal decisions on the basis of article 6 section 1 *Grundgesetz* (Constitution) and §134 *Bürgerliches Gesetzbuch* (Civil Law), and according to Swiss law on the basis of article 54 *Bundesverfassung* (Constitution) and article 20 *Obligationenrecht* (Law of obligations), no public or private employer, including the services, police or schoolboards, may legally insert a "celibacy clause" in the contract of employment.

priestly calling ties the hands of the church leadership not to reserve the priesthood to charismatic celibates only. For celibacy is not required, "what is expected of stewards is that each one should be found worthy of his trust" (1 Cor. 4:2) in passing on the word and grace of God to his people, as well as the demands of God and the apostles: no less, but also no more.

Chapter 6

The Sacraments of Ordination and Marriage are Reconcilable

Since the prohibition of marriage for priests developed historically out of a (partly) unconscious distaste for marriage, that is, out of heathen and Old Testament ideas on being polluted by the marital act of self-giving,[1] perhaps all the rational arguments so far adduced against the celibacy rules of the Latin Church will not prevail as long as the secret fear that priesthood and marriage might be basically irreconcilable[2] is not removed by strong arguments based on faith and the theology of sacrament.

1. *Christ was born from the Virgin's Womb*

A most impressive argument for the unconditional holiness of the so-called *membra ignorabilia* (1 Cor. 12:23) is provided by Christ himself, in that "when thou tookest upon thee to deliver man, thou didst *not* abhor the virgin's womb", as the *Te Deum* says. The virgin's womb was holy, not indeed because it was virgin but because it, like "everything created by God, is good" (1 Tim. 4:4). In other words, there was no reason to shrink from the womb. It was really only the composer of the *Te Deum* who did that, for reasons of his age, separated, not only

---

1. Pope Siricius above all expresses such ideas, see above, ch.2, n.4.
2. See above, Intro. n.14.

by centuries but by worlds, from the esteem in which the Shulammite bride was held in the Song of Solomon (1:9; 4:1–5, 1; 7:1–2).[3] Since the Son of Man chose to enter the world by way of "a woman's" (Gal 4:4) womb, then this way cannot be bad and impure or unholy on principle.

This is said more as general comment and still does not have any direct connection with the priesthood. But it may serve to remove the alleged general fear that the processes of procreation and birth are almost materially incompatible with God's holiness, which the priest has to represent in a special way. How many mothers up to our times, had to undergo the procedure of "churching" after having given birth to a child? The fact that this rite was cancelled by the church only a few decades ago shows how deeply these ritual norms inspired by unconscious fear of sexual affairs were rooted in the "collective mind" of cultic and cultural communities

Special arguments in favour of the compatibility of priestly ordination and marriage can be adduced, both from Christ's being the high priest – and therefore the model for all priests (Heb. 7–10) –, as also from the sacrament of marriage, the image of Christs's self-surrender to the Church.

2. *Christ is the Bridegroom and Husband of the Church*

No separate proof is needed to show that Christ is the high priest according to the Letter to the Hebrews, and that all New Testament priesthood as it has developed in

---

3. According to the encyclical *Divino afflante Spiritu* (DS 3826–30) the texts have, in the first place, to be taken in the literal sense.

the subsequent tradition is   only a sharing in Christ's priesthood, representing him. It does, however, need to be emphasized that Christ is or will be the husband, at latest when he returns at the consummation of the world. In the Revelation of John the angel says to the seer: "Come here and I will show you the Bride that the Lamb has married" (21:9). In a similar earlier image, the voice of the great multitude cries: "This is the time for the marriage of the Lamb. His Bride is ready" (19:7); she is "as beautiful as a bride all dressed for her husband" (21:2).

Of course these are images. But images do mean something and there is a reality behind these. They are found already in the Gospels: the parables of the royal wedding feast (Matt. 22:1–14 par) and of the ten virgins awaiting the Bridegroom (of all!, Matt. 25:1–13), both portraying Christ as the bridegroom shortly before his wedding. John the Baptist calls Jesus the bridegroom to whom he brings the bride (John 3:29). The Letter to the Ephesians even represents the relationship of Christ to his church as a marriage already existing: becoming one flesh, according to Genesis 2:24, "is a great mystery, but I am saying it applies to Christ and the Church" (Eph. 5:32); that is to say there is between them, too, a union of love, of flesh and of life. St Ephrem the Syrian, boldly applies this to the eucharist, in a prayer used in a marriage rite of the Eastern Catholic church: "Christ, thou the husband, thou who gave thy wife, the church, thy flesh and blood in the supper-room, bless these two. . ."[4] In fact, according to the Letter to the Ephesians, the Church as "Christ's body" (5:23), is related to Christ

---

4. Quoted by A. Raes, *Le mariage dans les Eglises d'Orient* (Chevetogne, 1958) pp.12, 150.

in the same way as his bride or his wife to her husband.

So, if the priest is to represent Christ, then it is also a true imitation of his being the husband of his church when the priest's life is the sacramental copy of Christ's marriage covenant with his Church. He then represents Christ in two ways: as a priest he models Christ in his attitude as teacher, priest and shepherd; as a married man he represents Christ in his attitude of selfless love.

It may not be denied that for the *unmarried* man, the "care for the affairs of the Lord" (1 Cor. 7:32) and consequently for the community of the Lord comes "more easily", as Vatican II says.[5] Yet, it should be remembered that this same council implicitly stated the possibility for married persons, as well, to "cleave to Christ with undivided heart".

Indeed, the priest not blessed with the charism of celibacy, but with the corresponding one of marriage, can cleave to Christ and "love God with his whole heart, with all his strength, with his whole soul and with his whole mind", and so also his neighbour, *only* within marriage, because only the sacrament of marriage keeps him from becoming a cramped "dry stick".

Therefore, representation of Christ in priesthood and marriage cannot be incompatible, because both represent the same love of Christ by a sacrament.

Which representation and which love has to be given priority, in case of conflict, has been stated by the Lord in clear terms which are always to be followed with extreme rigour: "If anyone comes to me and does not hate his own father and mother and wife and children, yes, and even hate his own life, he cannot be my

---

5. Vatican II, PO 16, see above, ch.2, n.38.

disciple" (Luke 14:26). Matthew has, instead of "hate": "love less" (Matt. 10:37). It implies that while a disciple can "take his wife with him" (1 Cor. 9:5), need not "leave" her, he must nevertheless be capable of doing her, if necessary, as well as his the other relatives, a harm which from her side looks like hatred.[6]

In fact, "to leave" wife and children, is not a precondition of Christ for his disciples. "Hatred" is. Without this, one *cannot* be his disciple". However, a special *reward* is promised for "leaving" a wife. Christ says: "Truly, I say to you there is no man who has left house or wife[7] or brothers or parents or children for the sake of the Kingdom of God, who will not receive payment many times over in this present time, and in the world to come, eternal life" (Luke 18:29f). This is the way of those who have achieved maturity in marriage and have then been made apt for the greater, all-embracing love in the sole cause of the Kingdom of God. In no way are only priests and office-holders meant by this word of the Lord.[8]

---

6. On Luke 14:26 cf. J. Schmid, *Das Evangelium nach Lukas*: RNT 3 (Regensburg, 3rd ed. 1955) pp.247f: "Only someone capable of the radical and painful decision to put all natural human ties second to the commitment to Jesus can really be a disciple of Jesus. . The command to join him is more important and requires of the disciple, in the case of conflict, that even father and mother be regarded as enemies of God's cause".

7. Significantly left out of the list by Mark and Matthew (Mark 10:29; Matt. 19:29), possibly because of the preceding teaching of Jesus on the indissolubility of marriage.

8. On Luke 18:29 par Mark 10:29f cf. J. Schmid, *Das Evangelium nach Markus*: RNT 2 (Regensburg, 4th ed. 1958) p.197: "Jesus' answer is *general* and normative in nature. Luke brings a promise of reward directed *exclusively* to the twelve in another connection (22:28–30)".

3. *The Husband is surrendered to His Wife as Christ is to the Church*

Another bridge can be built between priesthood and marriage based on their character as sacraments. There must be a relation between such similar entities.

If we look more closely at the nature of marriage as defined by Trent, we will discover such an affinity to sacrifice that even the last unconscious doubts about its compatibility with priesthood will disappear. The foundation of the bridge between priesthood and marriage is the statement of the doctrine on sacraments in general in which all sacraments flow from Christ's sacrifice on the cross. Each in its own way represents the same fundamental reality.[9] This general statement is adapted by the Council of Trent to the sacrament of marriage: "The grace which is to sanctify the marriage partners has been earned for us by Christ through his suffering; he gives and fulfills the venerable sacraments. The apostle Paul indicates that with the words: 'Husbands, love your wives, as Christ loved the Church and gave himself up for her'" (Eph 5:25).[10] The council sees the source of the grace which the marriage partners receive in the self-abandonment of Christ on the cross. The sign of this self-

---

9. Cf. the Tridentine sentences in DS 1529): "*Huius iustificationis causae sunt:. . meritoria: dilectissimus Unigenitus suus, qui sua sanctissima passione in ligno crucis nobis iustificationem meruit*" and DS 1600: "*. . de sanctissimis Ecclesiae sacramentis, per quae omnis vera iustitia vel incipit, vel coepta augetur vel amissa reparatur*": Christ has won for us all righteousness on the cross, and this justice is augmented or repaired by the sacraments.

10. Trent, DS 1799: "*Gratiam vero, quae coniuges sanctificaret, ipse Christus, venerabilium sacramentorum institutor atque perfector, sua passione nobis promeruit. Quod Paulus apostolus innuit dicens: 'Viri, diligite uxores vestras, sicut Christus dilexit Ecclesiam, et seipsum tradidit pro ea'*".

abandonment, a sign full of sacramentality, is the love of a husband abandoning himself to his wife.

Christ's sacrificing of his body on the cross – and the husbands' dedication of his body within marriage, are thus regarded by Paul and Trent as similar, even indeed as the original and the sacramental copy of the same thing: the conjugal self-dedication of the husband is a real sacramental copy of Christ's self-abandonment on the cross. It is permeated by it like the dough by the leaven. It represents the cross.[11]

This interpretation of the Tridentine dogmatical chapter does not overstretch matters. We are, indeed, allowed to include the dedication of the body into the nature of Christian marriage, since canon law on marriage does so, as well: "The marriage contract is an act of will by which both partners hand over (*tradit*) and receives (*acceptat*) the continuing and exclusive right over their body with regard to the acts which are, of themselves, apt to produce offspring".[12] The body is, according to the law, the object of the transferred right. The bodily acts belong to the nature of the sacrament. A *matrimonium non consummatum* is not a typical or normal marriage. The fact that the body belongs to the symbolic nature of sacraments is a consequence of God's incarnation in Christ. The Word of God became flesh, which continues in the Church, Christ's "body". So, too, sexuality, the

---

11. Cf. O.Casel, author of the "mystery-theory", quoted by M. Schmaus, *Katholische Dogmatik* IV,1 (Munich, 1952), pp.34, 37, 44ff: "Christ's unique death and unique resurrection become present to the recipient of the sacraments".

12. Can. 1081 no.2 CIC/1918; the new Code has instead: "Man and woman mutually surrender themselves, *sese mutuo tradunt*" (can. 1057, 2), which means: with body and soul, because in another canon it stresses the body: *coniugalem actum per se aptum ad prolis generationem* (can. 1061 §1 CIC/1983).

most "fleshly" component of the human body, can and shall "all be leavened" (Luke 13:21) with the leaven of faith and grace. *Quod non est assumptum, non est redemptum*, the church Fathers said.

We can draw a line from *"Christus tradidit se"* in Ephesians to the doctrinal chapter of Trent with its quotation of *"tradidit"*, and to the *"tradit"* in the legal definition of marriage in the Code: the essence of marriage in Christian understanding is self-surrender. This makes the sacraments of priesthood and marriage compatible. Christ's self-abandonment and conjugal self-giving both show that love goes as far as to sacrifice the body. Just as Christ has become one who is continually surrendered to his wife, the Church, through the crucifixion and its representation in the eucharistic bread, *"quod pro vobis tradetur"* (1 Cor. 11:24), the husband, through the marriage contract which aims at the giving of his body to his wife, has become one who is continually surrendered to his wife. In the deepest sense, this is a sacrifice, the renunciation of one's own authority over oneself, as Paul states: "The wife has no rights over her own body; it is the husband who has them. In the same way, the husband has no rights over his body; the wife has them" (1 Cor. 7:4). Marriage is, by its nature as a sacrament, a sharing in the cross of Christ. It is a *memoriale mortis domini* as is every other sacrament.[13]

The "permitted delights" about which much was said in earlier ecclesiastical usage[14] thus play, in the totality of the sacramental reality of marriage, a much smaller role

---

13. Cf n.9 above.
14. Cf. e.g. the encyclical of Pius XI, *Ad catholici sacerdotii fastigium*: AAS 28 (1936) 28: ". . *gaudiis atque solaciis quae in alio vitae instituto honeste capessere possunt"*.

than is commonly attributed to them. Schmaus comments: "Mutual subordination to one another means fellowship with Christ under the cross in mutual service to each other."[15]

The marital act involves, by its nature, all the forces of mind and soul – Holy Scripture calls it a "knowing"(!) –, therefore a self-surrender comparable to Christ's total self-sacrifice is possible and attainable. Of course, this way of self-sanctification through selfless giving, not selfish taking, has to be preached, proclaimed, demonstrated, otherwise no one knows the way. For instance, the wedding rite should be reformed, so as to say not: "I *take* you as my wife. . my husband" but "I *give* myself unto you as your husband. . your wife". It would indicate a "Copernican revolution" in Christian marriage, right from the beginning. Besides, Christian couples could be invited to pray before coming together, as Tobit and Sarah prayed before sleeping the first night together (Tob. 8:4–9). The grace used before meals is appropriate also before marital love: thanksgiving (1 Tim. 4:4–5).

If the celebrated *theologumenon* of the church Fathers that the church originated in a similar way from the open side of the second Adam, Christ, as did Eve from the side of the first Adam holds good,[16] then Christ's self-abandonment on the cross and the husband's self-abandonment in marriage are also similar to each other, in that as Christ's act founded the church, so the marital act founds the family. The family is often called "the litttle church". Scripture agrees: "If a man does not know

15. M. Schmaus, *Dogmatik* V,1 p.648.
16. Cf. e.g. M.-J. Scheeben, *Die Mysterien des Christentums* (new ed. by J. Hoefer, Freiburg, 1951) pp.156f.

how to manage his own household, how can he have care for God's church?" (1 Tim. 3:5). The letter to Timothy is right in comparing the duties of a father of a family and a pastor: even if this does not mean that every pastor *has to* have a family, the writer still provides the solution to our question of compatibility: not only do priesthood and marriage not rule each other out, but the family *can* even be good training for the office of pastor.[17]

The compatibility of the two sacraments of marriage and priesthood has been officially admitted by the popes, since they have, from 1951 onwards, given dispensations for converted married pastors, be they Protestant, Anglican or Old Catholic. All of them have been ordained to the Catholic priesthood: more than fifty in the United States alone. This shows that there is no theoretical problem for the Church at all in combining the two sacraments. And it is hard for the Vatican authorities to limit these "pastoral provisions" to converted clergy only, since the needs of communities deprived of a pastor are growing steadily.[18]

---

17. Cf. J. Roloff, *Der erste Brief an Timotheus*: Evangelisch-Katholischer Kommentar zum Neuen Testament 15 (Neunkirchen -Einsiedeln, 1988) p.160: "A prophet wandering about and without family ties, according to this view, would not be suitable as a leader of the community".
18. Cf. J.H. Fichter SJ, *The Pastoral Provisions – Married Catholic Priests* (Kansas City, 1990), and his second book on the issue: *The Wives of Catholic Clergy* (Kansas City, 1991).

Chapter 7

Celibate and Married Ministers have One Aim: Love

If the Church were to open the floodgates for the apostolic right of priests to marry, so far withheld, there would be some danger of destroying existing internal structures, such as the commonly shared vision of the ideal virgin priest, which Ida Friederike Görres has so movingly portrayed in her "Lay thoughts on celibacy"[1]. Yet preparatory steps towards a change have already been taken to accustom the laity to a married clergy, by the reintroduction of married deacons who officiate at the altar in priestly robes wearing their wedding ring, and through closer ecumenical relations with churches that have married priests. Also, the discussion about admission of *viri probati*, married men of proven character, to the priesthood in the Latin Church, has for some time prepared for the opening of the floodgates. Recent polls all over the world show that a great majority of Catholics (80 percent) would accept a married priesthood.

Nevertheless, the ordination of *viri probati* would be only a half-measure, because those priests for whom the way via marriage into the priesthood had not been

---

1. I. F. Görres, *Laiengedanken zum Zölibat* (Frankfurt, 2nd ed. 1962) pp.18–52. She does recognize the necessity of the charism for the maintenance of the virgin way of life, but she does not pay sufficient attention to the possible non-availability of this charism, which cannot simply be associated with the priestly vocation.

previously available when they were ordained, could in retrospect complain of unjust treatment. Even more so those priests dispensed from their obligations for marrying who then could really not understand why the combination of priesthood and marriage was not permitted for them, whereas it was now being made possible for others. The temporal succession of sacraments – be it marriage after priesthood or priesthood after marriage – certainly cannot be a serious reason for such discrimination.[2]

Therefore, it is a legitimate desire that the papal authority should opt for a courageous and at the same time level-headed granting of the sacrament of marriage to all those priests who have not received the charism of celibacy but the other charism of marriage (1 Cor. 7:7).[3] The unconscious fear that sexuality freed from prohibition could destroy church structures,[4] might be tempered by the faith which assures us that the sacramental grace of marriage will channel the forces of nature. The sacrament of marriage enables us to transform sexual power into personal love. Human maturity of men and women ripened through public marriage, in any case is to be preferred to hidden liaisons of the sort recently brought into the open by Press exposure of the fact that

---

2. See above, ch.3, n.35, the proposal by Patriarch Athenagoras to admit marriage after ordination.

3. Cf. R. Egenter, "Erwägungen zum Pflichtzölibat der katholischen Priester", *Stimmen der Zeit* 195 (1977) 635–8, and the reply by Joseph Cardinal Ratzinger, "Zum Zölibat der katholischen Priester", *ibid.* 781–3: he, however, does not base himself on the biblical notion of charism as set out in my chapter 1.

4. A Vatican spokesman, on one occasion, said to the author: "If the Church were to change the celibacy law, everything would collapse" – "crollerebbe tutto" (Interview with Mgr Mario Canciani, consultor to the Congregation for the Clergy, on 25 Feb. 1985).

the Bishop of Galway had a seventeen-year-old son.[5] The Lord has said, especially with a view to office-holders: "Beware of the leaven of Pharisees, that is hypocrisy." (Luke 12,1). The exodus of so many faithful from the Church is certainly due, at least to some extent, to a loss of credibility, since the unability of many priests for celibacy has become evident.

Love is the meaning of life, and nobody must be ashamed of it. Love is the aim of Christian teaching: "The only purpose of this instruction is that there should be love, coming out of a pure heart" (1 Tim. 1:5). The reason for this to be our purpose is simple: "God is love" (1 John 4:8, 16), and "when he appears we shall be like him" (1 John 3:2). We shall be judged in accordance with love: "What you did to the least of my brethren, you did it to me" (cf. Matt. 25:31–46); we shall be asked about our wedding garment (Matt. 22:12).

Love, the essence of which consists in self-giving, cannot be divided into – basically different – love of God or love of our neighbour. In the apostle Paul's hymn of love (1 Cor. 13), divine and human love cannot be separated from one another. And according to the Letter to the Ephesians (5:22–33) husbands are to love their wives with a love like that of Christ for his Church. Therefore, sacramental conjugal love should and can be a legitimate school and expression of the love needed for being a disciple of Christ.

If, at the same time as instruction is given on Christ-like marital love, the ideal of virginity is propagated, so that the charism of celibacy granted according to Matthew 19:11f is discovered and fostered, then the bursting of the dam, with disastrous effects on the faith

---

5. Cf. *The Observer* (London), 10 May 1992, p.4.

and spirituality of both priests and laity, need not be feared and the missing 20 percent will accept married priests, as well. A decisive phrase in this direction has been uttered by Pope John Paul II himself, in one of his addresses on marriage given during the year 1982: "The words of the Gospel of St Matthew (19,11 and 19,29) do not furnish arguments to affirm either an inferiority of marriage or a superiority of virginity or celibacy... The measure of Christian perfection is love".[6]

The recommendation of charismatic celibacy can, therefore, only be made taking into account the different charisms which different individuals receive from God (1 Cor. 7:7). It would have to start from the exegetical datum that only those who have received the charism of celibacy are able to transform their sexual creative force, which is implanted in them as well into personal love, *without* a marriage partner, thanks to the grace of God which protects them from tension and illness. Sublimation for the Kingdom of God presupposes grace, not only good will and intention. Of course their charism too may be subject to temptations, since they are not physically "impotent" but only spiritually "unable to marry" on account of the greater love for God by whom "this (ability) is given" (Matt. 19:11). Yet the meaning of "charism" is that it is easy for them to resist the temptations. Against this, others would give way to it, for the simple reason that God has given to them "the other gift" of vocation to marriage (1 Cor. 7:7). They for their part can transform the potential of bodily love only by means of the "generator" called the sacrament of marriage, into "warmth" and "light", that is, into the

---

6. General Audience of 14 April 1982, *Osservatore Romano* 15 Apr.1982.

more sublime forms of personal love. Yet, for married persons and celibates there is one aim: love in and for Christ.

The final event of our ripening process on earth, which the Lord so often describes in the image of the growing and ripening seed, is, indeed, the same for all: we are called "to seek God and to find him" (Acts 17:27), and, at our second birth, at death, to "see him as he is" (1 John 3:2), "face to face" (1 Cor. 13:12), and to encounter a love which far exceeds every earthly love, even in marriage: the love of *the* Bridegroom (Matt. 22:2; Rev. 21:2). Marriage, however, is allowed to be a model of this love. At the wedding-feast of the Lamb (Rev. 19:7.9), the Church will become his "Wife" (Rev. 21:2, 9). Then he wants to give us his own love – divine love –, and his own life – eternal life. That is the amazing news which priests have to proclaim "in every way" (Phil. 1:18), whether within or outside marriage. God loves each of his creatures (Wisd. 11:25), and God can be reached from all states of life. For, marriage as well as celibacy are "gifts of grace", "charisms" coming "from God" (1 Cor. 7:7), for which everyone who has received them must thank God from the bottom of an undivided heart.

Bibliography

Abbot, W., ed. *The Documents of Vatican II*. Washington, DC and London, 1966.

Acta Apostolicae Sedis (AAS) 1908ff.

Allo, E.-B., "Première Epître aux Corinthiens," *Etudes Bibliques*. Paris, 2nd ed. 1956.

Alvaro del Portillo, "Caelibatus sacerdotalis in Decreto conciliario *Presbyterorum Ordinis*," *Seminarium* (Rome) 19 (1967) 711–28.

Baltensweiler, H., "Die Ehe im Neuen Testament. Exegetische Untersuchungen über Ehe, Ehelosigkeit und Ehescheidung," *Abhandlungen zur Theologie des Alten und Neuen Testaments* 52. Zürich-Stuttgart, 1967.

Bauer, J.B., "Uxores circumducere (1 Kor 9,5)," *Biblische Zeitschrift (Neue Folge)* 3 (1959) 94–102.

Bauer, W., *Griechisch-Deutsches Wörterbuch zu den Schriften des Neuen Testaments und der übrigen urchristlichen Literatur*. Berlin, 5th ed. 1958.

Bertrams, W., "De voto castitatis clericorum saecularium," *Periodica de re morali canonica liturgica* 44 (1955) 139–74.

Idem, "De caelibatu clericorum," *Periodica* 50 (1961) 204–11.

Idem, "Priestertum, Jungfräulichkeit und Keuschheitsgelübde in ihren theologischen Beziehungen," *Geist und Leben* 28 (1955) 95–104.

Idem, Der Zölibat des Priesters. Würzburg, 2nd ed. 1962.

Blinzler, J., "Eisìn eunoûchoi. Zur Auslegung von Mt 19,12," *Zeitschrift für die neutestamentliche Wissenschaft* 48 (1957) 254–70.

Brox, N., *Die Pastoralbriefe: Regensburger Neues Testament* (RNT) 7,2. Regensburg, 4th ed. 1969.

Cholij, R., *Clerical Celibacy in East and West*. Leominster, 1989.

Clement of Alexandria, *Paedagogos*. PG 8, 247–684; GCS 1, 89–292.

Idem, Stromata. PG 8, 895 – PG 9, 602; GCS 2.

Clement, R., *Dialoghi con Atenagora.* Turin, 1972.

Codex Iuris Canonici. Vatican City, 1983.

Codex Iuris Canonici. Vatican City, 1917.

Conciliorum Oecumenicorum Decreta, ed. J. Alberigo, P.P. Joannou, C. Leonardi et P. Prodi. Freiburg, 1962; Bologna, 3rd ed. 1973.

Concilium Tridentinum. Diariorum, Actorum, Epistularum, Tractatuum Nova Collectio (CT) 9. Freiburg, 1924.

Congregatio de sacramentis, Instructio of 27.12.1930, Appendix, Declaratio propria manu subscribenda a candidatis in singulis sacris Ordinibus suscipendis, iuramento coram Ordinario praestito. AAS 23 (1930) 127.

Congregatio pro Doctrina Fidei, Normae ad apparandas in Curiis dioecesanis et religiosis causas reductionis ad statum laicalem cum dispensatione ab obligationibus cum sacra Ordinatione conexis, 13.1.1971. AAS 63 (1971) 303–8.

Cornely, R., "Commentarius in S. Pauli Apostoli Epistulas 2, Prior Epistula ad Corinthios," *Cursus Scripturae Sacrae.* Paris, 1890.

Corpus Iuris Canonici, ed Ae. Friedberg, 1–2. Leipzig, 1879; reprint Graz, 1955.

Declais, J.-L., "Réponse au synode des évêques (1990)," *Jésus* (Paris-Damville) 3/1991, 32–5.

Denzinger, H.- Schönmetzer, A., *Enchiridion Symbolorum et Declarationum de Rebus Fidei et Morum* (DS). Barcelona-Freiburg-Rome, 34th ed. 1967 (Editions before 1962: D).

Denzler, G., *Das Papsttum und der Amtszölibat 1–2, Päpste und Papsttum 5,1–2* (Stuttgart) 1973–6.

Documentation catholique (Paris) 2017, 9.2.1990.

Dupont, J., *Mariage et Divorce dans l'Evangile.* Bruges, 1959.

Eusebius of Caesarea, *Historia Ecclesiastica,* Migne, PG 20.

Fichter, J., *The Pastoral Provisions – Married Catholic Priests.* Kansas City, 1990.

Idem, The Wives of Catholic Clergy. Kansas City, 1991.

Funk, F.X., *Didascalia et Constitutiones Apostolorum.* Paderborn, 1905 (reprint).

Galot, J., "Lo stato di vita degli apostoli," *La Civiltà cattolica* 3346, 18.11.1989.

Gesenius, W., *Hebräisches und Aramäisches Handwörterbuch über das Alte Testament.* Leipzig, 17th ed. 1915; reprint Berlin, 1959, 1962.

Goldmann-Posch, U., *Unheilige Ehen.* Munich, 1989.

Häring, B., *Das Gesetz Christi* 1–3. Freiburg, 6th ed. 1961. Eng. trans. *The Law of Christ.* Westminster, Md., 1961.

Hatch, E. and H. Redpath, *Concordance to the Septuagint* 2. Oxford, 1897.

Hilary of Poitiers, *Tractatus super Psalmos.* PL 9, 231–890; CSEL 22.

Höffner, J., "Um des Himmelreiches willen. Über den Zölibat der Priester. Zehn Thesen des Erzbischofs von Köln," *Themen und Thesen* 1. Cologne, 6th ed. 1975.

Horace, *Epistulae* I.

Jedin, H., *Geschichte des Konzils von Trient* 4,2. Freiburg, 1975.

Jeremias, J., *Die Abendmahlsworte Jesu.* Göttingen, 4th ed. 1966. Eng. trans. *The Eucharistic Words of Jesus.* London and New York, 1966.

Jerome, *De perpetua virginitate beatae Mariae adversus Helvidium.* Migne PL 23 (1883) 194–215.

Idem, Adversus Jovinianum. PL 123 (1883) 222–352.

Idem, Epistula 22 ad Eustochium. PL 22 (1877) 394–425; CSEL 54, 143–211.

Jone, H., *Das Gesetzbuch der lateinischen Kirche* 2. Paderborn, 2nd ed. 1952.

Jülicher, A., *Die Gleichnisreden Jesu* 1. Tübingen, 2nd ed. 1910.

Kertelge, K., *Gemeinde und Amt im Neuen Testament.* Munich, 1972.

Kittel, G. (Ed.), *Theologisches Wörterbuch zum Neuen Testament.* Stuttgart, 1933ff.

Klauck, H.-J., *1. Korintherbrief: Neue Echterbibel.* Würzburg, 1984.

Kottje, R., "Das Aufkommen der täglichen Eucharistiefeier in der Westkirche und die Zölibatsgesetzgebung," *Zeitschrift für Kirchengeschichte* 82 (1971) 218–28.

Kümmel, W.G., *An die Korinther I.II: Handbuch zum Neuen Testament* 9. Tübingen, 5th ed. 1969.

Kürzinger, J., "Die Briefe an die Korinther und Galater," *Echterbibel* (NT) 4. Würzburg, 1954.

Kuss, O., *Die Briefe an die Römer, Korinther und Galater: RNT* 6. Regensburg, 1940.

Lagrange, M.-J., *Evangile selon Matthieu: Etudes Bibliques*. Paris, 8th ed. 1948.

Lang, F., *Die Briefe an die Korinther: Das Neue Testament Deutsch (NTD)* 7. Göttingen-Zürich, 1986.

Lawrence, C.H., "Unconvincing Arguments against a Married Priesthood," *The Tablet* (London) 6.1.1990, 14.

Lederer, J., "Rezension zu W. Bertrams, Der Zölibat des Priesters," *Archiv für katholisches Kirchenrecht* 129 (1959/60) 668–70.

Leist, F., *Zum Thema Zölibat. Bekenntnisse von Betroffenen*. Munich, 1973.

Lexikon für Theologie und Kirche, 2nd edition, 1–10. Freiburg, 1957–1965.

Lidell, H.G. and R. Scott, *A Greek-English Lexicon*. Oxford, 9th ed. 1966.

Mansi, J.D., *Sacrorum Conciliorum Nova et Amplissima Collectio* 21. Venedig, 1726; reprint Paris, 1903.

Marchal, L., "Evangile selon Saint Luc," *La Sainte Bible* (Pirot-Clamer). Paris, 2nd ed. 1950.

Mattino, Il, 30.8.1991.

Maximos IV. Saigh, "Priestertum, Zölibat und Ehe in der Ostkirche," *Der Seelsorger* (Vienna) 87 (1967) 302–6.

Meigne, M., "Concile ou Collection d'Elvire?," *Revue d'histoire ecclésiastique* 70 (1975) 361–87.

Migne, J.P., *Patrologia, Series Graeca* (PG); *Series Latina* (PL).

Mörsdorf, K., *Lehrbuch des Kirchenrechts* 1. Paderborn, 11th ed. 1964.

Müller, M., *Die Lehre des hl. Augustinus von der Paradiesesehe und ihre Auswirkung in der Sexualethik des 12. und 13. Jahrhunderts bis Thomas von Aquin: Studien zur Geschichte der katholischen Moral-theologie* 1. Regensburg, 1954.

Niederwimmer, K., *Askese und Mysterium. Über Ehe, Eheschei-dung und Eheverzicht in den Anfängen des christlichen Glaubens: Forschungen zur Religion und Literatur des Alten und Neuen Testaments* 113. Göttingen, 1975.

Nötscher, F., *Die Psalmen: Echterbibel* (AT) 4. Würzburg, 2nd ed. 1959.

Observer, The, (London) 10.5.1992, 4.

Osservatore Romano (Rome) 1975, 1982, 1985.

Paul VI., Encyclical *Sacerdotalis caelibatus*. AAS 59 (1967) 657–97.

Idem, Motuproprio, 15.8.1972. AAS 64 (1972) 534–40.

Pius XI., Encyclical *Ad catholici sacerdotii fastigium.* AAS 28 (1936) 5–53.

Idem, Encyclical *Casti conubii* AAS 22 (1930) 539–92.

Pius XII, Encyclical *Sacra virginitas.* AAS 46 (1954) 161–91.

Pontificale Romanum. Rome, 1972.

Quesnel, Q., "Made themselves eunuchs for the Kingdom of Heaven (Mt 19,12)," *Catholic Biblical Quarterly* 30 (1968) 335–58.

Raes, A., *Le mariage dans les Eglises d'Orient.* Chevetogne, 1958.

Rice, D., *Shattered Vows. Exodus from the Priesthood.* London, 1990; Belfast, 3rd ed. 1991.

Roloff, J., *Der erste Brief an Timotheus: Evangelisch-Katholischer Kommentar* 15. Neunkirchen-Einsiedeln, 1988.

Sabatier, P., *Vetus Italica.* Reims 1743–49; Paris, 2nd ed. 1751.

Schäfer, K.Th., *Grundriss der Einleitung in das Neue Testament.* Bonn, 2nd ed. 1952.

Scheeben, M.-J., *Die Mysterien des Christentums,* new ed. by J. Höfer. Freiburg, 1951.

Schillebeeckx, E., *Der Amtszölibat. Eine kritische Besinnung: Theologische Perspektiven.* Düsseldorf, 1967.

Schlier, H., "Die Ordnung der Kirche nach den Pastoralbriefen," *Zeit der Kirche. Exegetische Aufsätze und Vorträge.* Freiburg, 1965, 129–47.

Schmaus, M., *Katholische Dogmatik* 45, 1. Munich, 1952.

Schmid, J., *Das Evangelium nach Matthäus: RNT* 1. Regensburg, 4th ed. 1959.

Idem, Das Evangelium nach Markus: RNT 2. Regensburg, 4th ed. 1958.

Idem, Das Evangelium nach Lukas: RNT 3. Regensburg, 3rd ed. 1955.

Seibel, W., "Die vierte Sitzungsperiode des Konzils," *Stimmen der Zeit* 177 (1966) 45–63.

Sipe, R., *A Secret World. Sexuality and the Search for Celibacy.* New York, 1990.

Spicq, C., *Epîtres aux Corinthiens: La Sainte Bible* (Pirot- Clamer) 11b. Paris, 1951.

Strathmann, H., *Der Brief an die Hebräer: Das Neue Testament Deutsch* 9. Göttingen, 6th ed. 1953, 68–158.

Suitbertus a S. Joanne a Cruce, Book Review of H.-J. Vogels, *Untersuchungen zur Bedeutung des Verses 1 Kor 9,5* (Ettal 1961). *Ephemerides Carmeliticae* 12 (Rome, 1961), 476–8.

Tertullian, *De exhortatione castitatis. Corpus Scriptorum Ecclesiasticorum Latinorum* (CSEL) 70, 125–52; *Corpus Christianorum* (CC) 2, 1015–35.

Idem, De monogamia. CSEL 76, 44–78; CC 2, 1229–53.

Idem, De pudicitia. CSEL 20, 219–73; CC 2, 1281–330.

Thurian, M., *Ehe und Ehelosigkeit, zwei Dienstordnungen christlichen Lebens.* Gelnhausen-Berlin, undated.

Van Hove, A., *Commentarium Lovaniense in Codicem Iuris Canonici 1,1. Prolegomena.* Malines-Rome, 2nd ed. 1945.

Vetus Latina. Die Reste der altlateinischen Bibel. By Petrus Sabatier, ed. by Monks of the Erzabtei Beuron. Freiburg, 1949.

Vogels, H.-J., *Untersuchungen zur Bedeutung des Verses 1 Kor 9,5.* (Privately printed Ettal, 1961). Port. trans. "O sentido de 1 Corintios 9,5," *Atualidades Biblicas. Miscelânea em memória de Frei Joâo José Pedreira de Castro OFM,*" ed. by J. Salvador. Petrópolis, 1971, 558–71.

Idem, "Le mogli degli apostoli," *Vita Pastorale* (Alba) 78 (1990), Vol. 11, 56–7.

Weinkauff, H., "Widerstandsrecht," *Staatslexikon,* ed. by the Görresgesellschaft, 8. Freiburg, 6th ed. 1963, 677–83.

Wendland, H.D., *Die Briefe an die Korinther:* NTD 7. Göttingen, 12th ed. 1968.

Wili, H.U., "Zur Zölibatspflicht der Weltkleriker im katholischen Kirchenrecht," *Theologische Berichte* 4. Cologne-Einsiedeln-Zürich, 1974.

Wordsworth, J. and H.I. White, *Novum Testamentum Domini nostri Jesu Christi Latine secundum Editionem Sancti Hieronymi.* Oxford, 1913ff.

Zimmermann, H., *Neutestamentliche Methodenlehre.* Stuttgart, 3rd ed. 1970.

Zuntz, G., *The Text of the Epistles.* London, 1953.